MacBo

User Guide

The Beginner to Advanced Guide of Boosting your Productivity with MacBook Pro & MacOS Catalina

Important

1. p.22 See your Stuff.
2. p.88 Create documents.
3. p.90 Save a document.

Raphael Stone

Contents

Chapter 1 - MacOS Catalina Basics:

Chapter 2 - Maximizing the Apps:

Chapter 3 - Customize your Mac:

Chapter 4 - Work with Files and Folders:

Chapter 5 - Apple ID and iCloud:

Chapter 6 - Family and Friends:

Chapter 7 - Use Your Apple Devices together:

Chapter 8 - Music, TV, Books, News and more:

Chapter 9 - Privacy and Security:

Chapter 10 - Mac Hardware:

Introduction

There is a lot to love in Apple's latest pro-level portable Macs. The new 13-inch MacBook Pro with Touch Bar looks identical to its predecessor, but once you start using it, you'll feel the difference in multiple ways. It also offers new features that seem subtle on the surface (like Hey Siri and a True Tone display) but, surprisingly, make a big difference in everyday use. Add in an improved keyboard, and you have what looks like a winner.

Apple has provided its beloved MacBook Pro 13 with 4 Thunderbolt 3 ports, an updated processor, as well as a revised Butterfly keyboard.

With the sixteenth version of Apple's MacOS, **MacOS Catalina 10.15** was released earlier this month on October 7th. It is expected that Apple will be shipping all new Mac machines with MacOS Catalina 10.15. In terms of support, Catalina will run on all machines that ran Mojave (the previous named version), except for Mac Pros released between 2010 and 2012. This book will teach all all the tips and tricks to master your MacBook Pro using the new MacOS Catalina.

Chapter 1 MacOS Catalina Basics

What's in the menu bar on Mac?

The menu bar runs along the top of the screen on your Mac. Use the menus and icons in the menu bar to choose commands, perform tasks, and check status.

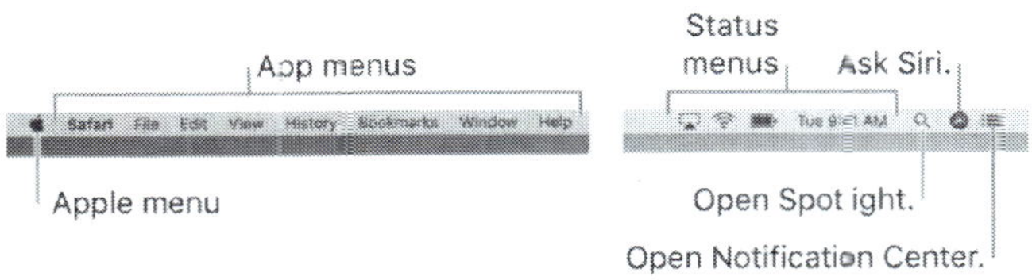

You can set an option in General preferences to automatically hide the menu bar; then it's shown only when you move the pointer to the top of the screen.

Apple menu

The Apple menu , located in the top-left corner of the screen, contains commands for things you do frequently, such as update apps, open System Preferences, lock your screen, or shut down your Mac.

App menus

App menus are located next to the Apple menu. The name of the app you're using appears in bold, followed by other menus, often with standard names such as File, Edit, Format, or Window. Each app has a Help menu to make it easy to get information about using an app...

Each menu contains commands, many of which are available in most apps. For example, the Open command is often in the File menu. For information about the symbols in the menu commands,

Status menus

Toward the right end of the menu bar are *status menus*, typically represented by icons. Use these menus to check the status of your Mac or quickly access features—for example, quickly turn Wi-Fi on or off or check your computer's battery charge.

You can add status menus, such as the emoji viewer or a volume control icon. You can also add status menus for some apps when you install them.

To rearrange the status menu icons, press and hold the Command key while dragging the items. To remove an icon, press and hold the Command key and drag the icon out of the menu bar.

Spotlight

Click the Spotlight icon , located after the status menus, to use Spotlight to search for items on your Mac and more.

Siri

Following Spotlight is the Siri icon —click it to ask Siri to do things like open files or apps, or to find things on your Mac or on the internet. You can easily keep Siri results handy on your desktop or in Notification Center.

Notification Center

At the right end of the menu bar, click the Notification Center icon to use Notification Center to view details about your day and catch up on notifications you missed.

Search with Spotlight on Mac

Spotlight can find items on your Mac, show all kinds of information—from sources like the web, Maps, and Music—and even get conversions, calculations, and definitions for you.

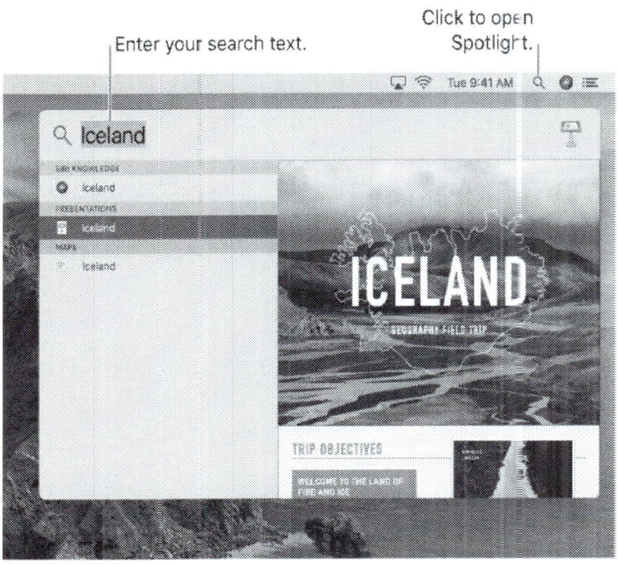

Tip: You can drag the Spotlight window anywhere on the desktop and make it bigger.

Search for something

1. On your Mac, click the Spotlight icon in the upper-right corner of the menu bar, or press Command-Space bar.

   If it's your first time using Spotlight, a description is shown in the Spotlight window and the search field says Spotlight Search.

2. In the search field, type what you're looking for—results appear as you type.

   - Find files on your Mac by typing what you're looking for in the same way you'd say it. For example, you could search by typing "California photos" or "emails from Kelly."
   - Find things on the web using Spotlight Suggestions and in the iTunes Store, the App Store, and Apple Books. For example, you can search for weather, sports, websites, stocks, flight status, celebrities, music, movies, books, and more.

View and use search results

- *Open an item:* Double-click an item in the results list on the left. Or select the item, then press the Return key.
- *Use a preview:* Click items or links in the preview on the right. For example, to hear a song in your music playlist, click the Play button next to the song.
- *Show the location of a file on your Mac:* Select the file in the results list, then press and hold the Command key to show the file's location at the bottom of the preview.
- *Copy an item:* Drag a file from the results list to the desktop or a Finder window.
- *See files recently used in an app:* Enter the app's name (don't press the Return key unless you want to open the app). To open a file, double-click it in the preview.
- *Make a desktop shortcut to an item:* Drag the item from the results list to the desktop; just click it on the desktop to open the item in the appropriate app, such as Safari.
- *See all results from your Mac in the Finder:* Scroll to the bottom of the results list, then double-click Show

all in Finder. You can narrow the results in the Finder.

During downtime, or if you reach the time limit set for apps in Screen Time preferences, app icons are dimmed and an hourglass icon is shown.

Get conversions, calculations, and definitions

- *Convert currencies:* Enter an amount to see the equivalent in other common currencies. For example, enter $100, £100, or ¥100. Or enter something like "300 krone in dollars."
- *Convert temperatures:* Enter a temperature like 98.8F or 32C. Or enter something like "340K in F."
- *Convert measurements:* Enter a measurement like 25 lb., 54 yards, or 23 stone. Or enter something like "32 ft. to meters."
- *Get a calculation:* Enter a mathematical expression, such as 956*23.94.
- *Get a definition:* Enter a word or phrase, then click the result in the Definition section.

Ask Siri. Say something like: "How many centimeters in an inch?" or "What does parboil mean?" When Spotlight Suggestions are enabled, some apps—for example, Mail, Messages, and Notes—may outline an item (such as an artist name, a place, or a movie title) in text or make it a link as a hint that more information is available. (Your messages, emails, and other content are not sent to Apple; only the items identified as Look up hints and related usage data may be sent.)

You can exclude specific folders, disks, or types of information (such as email or messages) from Spotlight searches. If you want Spotlight to search content only on your Mac and not include results from the web, you can turn off Spotlight Suggestions.

Use Siri on your Mac

Siri on your Mac can help you with everyday tasks, get quick answers and information, play music, and more. You can ask Siri so many things—from “Set up a meeting at 9” to “What was the score for last night’s game?” Siri is there to help.

Siri can make suggestions in some apps even before you ask. For example, when you receive invitations in Mail or book flights in Safari, Siri suggests adding them to your calendar. Or, when you browse webpages, Siri can suggest related webpages.

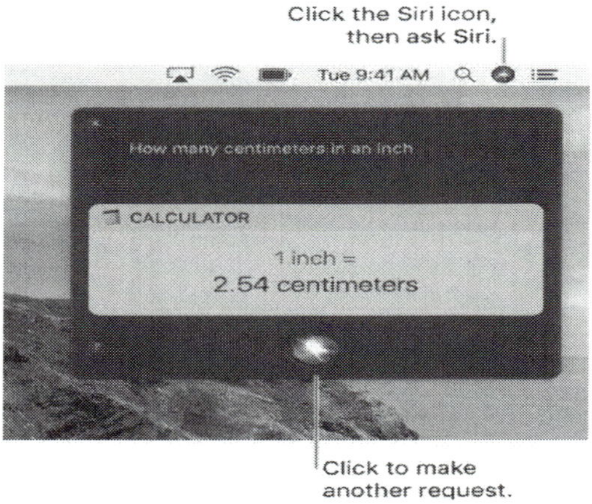

Ask Siri

To ask Siri on your Mac, do any of the following:

- Click the Siri icon in the menu bar (or use the Touch Bar.
- If your Mac supports it, say “Hey Siri.” Your portable computer must be open to use Hey Siri.

  If Siri doesn’t respond, open Siri preferences and make sure Listen for “Hey Siri” is turned on. You can also use Hey Siri when your supported Mac is locked or in sleep.
- If your connected Air Pods or supported headphones support it, say “Hey Siri.”

  If Siri doesn’t respond, open Siri preferences and make sure Listen for “Hey Siri” on Air Pods is turned on. You can also use Hey Siri when your Mac is locked.

Tip: When you use Siri, your device sends Apple information such as your name and nickname, or the names and nicknames of your contacts if you set these up in Contacts. This happens in order for Siri to understand you better and recognize what you say. Try it out by asking "What's my name?" Or, if you've added a work address, Siri can remind you to do things such as get groceries when you leave work.

Ways to use Siri

You can use Siri to get quick answers (say something like "What's the weather

Tomorrow?") Or do a task for you, like turn on Do Not Disturb.

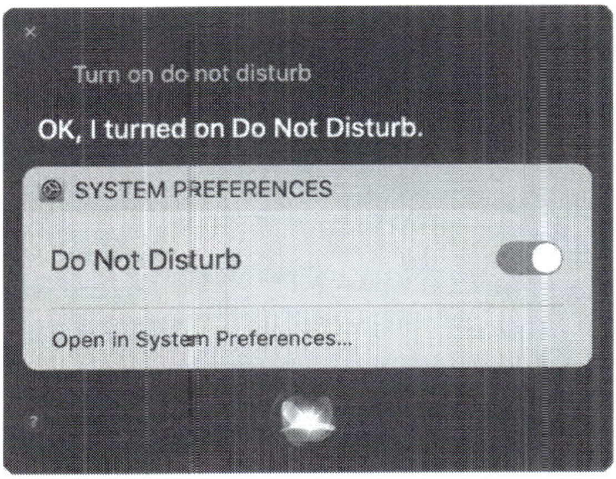

On your Mac, ask Siri a question or to do a task for you.

Here are some examples:

"Open Notes."

"Show me my passwords."

"Create a note" and then dictate what you want to write.

"Create a meeting for today at 3 p.m."

"Where's the nearest grocery store?" or "what's the weather tomorrow?"

Tip: Ask Siri "What can you do?" or click the Help button in the Siri window for even more ideas of how Siri can help you.

If you'd rather type your requests to Siri instead of speaking them, you can turn on Type to Siri. If the Siri window doesn't close automatically, you can close it yourself—just swipe right on your trackpad or click the Close button .

Use Siri results

You can keep Siri results handy in Notification Center or use them in emails or documents.

On your Mac, do any of the following:

- *Pin results to Notification Center:* If you see an Add button in the top-right corner of the results, click it to add the results to Today view in Notification Center.

The results stay pinned and are kept up to date until you remove them. You can pin many types of results, such as stock prices, sports schedules, and more.

- *Open a result:* Double-click a webpage to open it in Safari, or double-click a file or document to open it in the appropriate app on your Mac. A result to preview it in a Quick Look window.
- *Use or save a result:* Drag and drop to add images or locations into an email or document or to the desktop. (You can also copy or paste text.)

Troubleshoot Siri

If you're having trouble using Siri, try these solutions:

- Make sure your Mac is connected to the internet. Choose Apple menu > System Preferences, then click Network.
- Make sure Siri is turned on. Choose Apple menu > System Preferences, click Siri, then select Enable Ask Siri.
- Make sure your Mac has a microphone and that it's not obstructed by your clothing or body or other objects.

- If you're using an external microphone, check that it's connected to your Mac, selected under Input in Sound preferences, and that the mic's input volume is set high enough.

  Choose Apple menu > System Preferences, click Sound, click Input, and then drag the "Input volume" slider.

- If you're using Air Pods that support Hey Siri, make sure they're connected with your Mac. and the Apple Support article

- If you want to stop using Siri, choose Apple menu > System Preferences, click Siri, then deselect the Enable Ask Siri checkbox.

You can customize Siri—for example, change the voice Siri uses or the language Siri speaks.

Siri uses Location Services to provide information, services, and features appropriate to where you are. You can change the setting that allows Siri to do so. You can also use Siri on your Mac to control lights and other accessories in your home. And the Apple Support article

Use Notification Center on Mac

In Notification Center on your Mac, Today view shows details about your day—appointments, weather, birthdays, even a summary of what you have planned for tomorrow—and Notifications view shows notifications you missed.

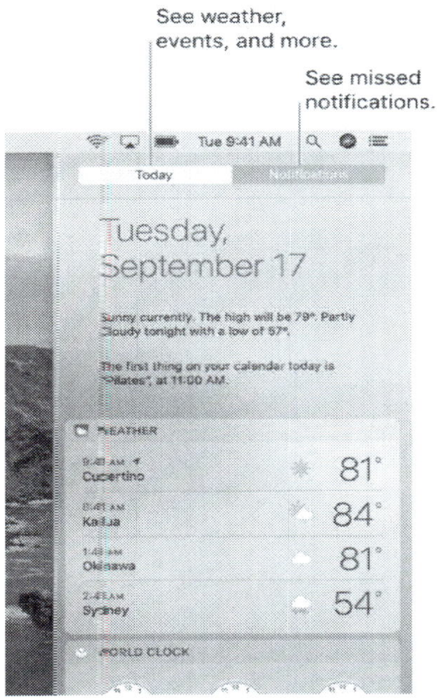

Tip: To customize or stop notifications, click the Notifications preferences icon in the bottom-right corner of Notification Center.

Use Today view in Notification Center

1. On your Mac, click the Notification Center icon in the menu bar, or swipe left with two fingers from the right edge of the trackpad.
2. In Notification Center, click today.

3. Click an item in a widget to see its details or take an action.

   For example, click an item in the Weather widget to show the hourly and five-day forecasts. Or click a reminder's checkbox to complete it.

Customize Today view Notification Center

1. On your Mac, click the Notification Center icon in the menu bar, or swipe left with two fingers from the right edge of the trackpad.
2. In Notification Center, click today.
3. Do any of the following:
   - *Customize a widget:* Move the pointer over the widget, then click the Info button that appears.
   - *Reorder widgets:* Click Edit at the bottom of Today view, then drag a widget up or down.
   - *Add or remove widgets:* Click Edit (or the new widget count, if shown) at the bottom of Today view. To add an available widget, click its Add button. To remove a widget, click

its Remove button ; the widget is moved to the list of available widgets.

Get more widgets: Click Edit at the bottom of Today view, click App Store, then buy or download widgets. For more information about buying and downloading items,

Use Notifications view in Notification Center

1. On your Mac, click the Notification Center icon in the menu bar, or swipe left with two fingers from the right edge of the trackpad.
2. In Notification Center, click Notifications.
3. Click a notification to open the item in the associated app. For example, click a Mail notification to open the email in Mail.

When you open an item, it's removed from Notifications view. To remove an item without opening it, move the pointer over it, then click the Clear button . Or click the button for a day to remove all of the day's notifications.

You can turn Night Shift and Do Not Disturb on or off in Notification Center—just swipe down, then click the button.

- When you turn on Night Shift, it stays on until midnight, sunrise, the next scheduled time to turn off (based on settings in Night Shift preferences), or you turn it off.

- When you turn on Do Not Disturb, it stays on until midnight, the next scheduled time to turn off (based on settings in Notifications preferences), or you turn it off.

  When Do Not Disturb is on, the Notification Center icon in the menu bar is dimmed. You don't see or hear notifications arrive; they are collected in Notification Center where you can view them later.

Get to know the Mac desktop

At the top of the screen is the menu bar and at the bottom is the Dock. In between is what's called the desktop. The desktop is where you do most of your work.

You can change the look of your desktop by customizing the desktop picture and by choosing a light or dark appearance for the menu bar, desktop picture, Dock, and built-in apps.

When you open an app, its windows appear over the desktop. If your desktop is covered with windows, you can use Mission Control to see a simple view of everything that's open so it's easy to spot the window you need. You can also create and work in additional desktop spaces.

If you like to keep files handy on the desktop, you can use stacks to neatly group them along one

Side of the desktop—whenever you add a file to the desktop, it automatically goes into a stack.

Use the Dock on Mac

The Dock on the Mac desktop is a convenient place to access apps and features (like Siri, Launchpad, and the Trash) that you're likely to use every day. The Dock can show up to three recently used apps that aren't already in the Dock and a folder for items you download from the internet.

Open items in the Dock

In the Dock on your Mac, do any of the following:

- *Open an app:* Click the app icon. For example, to open the Finder, click the Finder icon in the Dock.
- *Open a file in an app:* Drag the file over an app's icon. For example, to open a document you created in Pages, drag the document over the Pages icon in the Dock.
- *Show an item in the Finder:* Command-click the item's icon.

- *Switch to the previous app and hide the current app:* Option-click the current app's icon.
- *Switch to another app and hide all other apps:* Option-Command-click the icon of the app you want to switch to.

You can Control-click an item to display a shortcut menu of other actions to take, such as open or close an app, open a recent document, and more.

If an app stops responding, you can Force Quit the app from the Dock (you may lose unsaved changes). Control-Option-click the app's icon, then choose Force Quit.

Add or remove Dock items

On your Mac, do any of the following:

- *Add an item to the Dock:* Drag apps to the left side of (or above) the line that separates the recently used apps. Drag files and folders to the right side of (or below) the other line that separates recently used apps. An alias for the item is placed in the Dock.

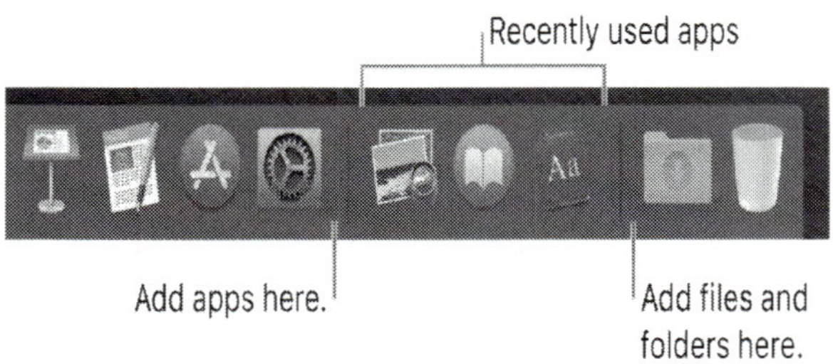

- *Remove an item from the Dock:* Drag the item out of the Dock until you see Remove. Only the alias is removed; the actual item remains on your Mac.

  If you accidentally remove an app icon from the Dock, it's easy to put it back (the app is still on your Mac). Open the app to make its icon appear again in the Dock. Control-click the app's icon, then choose Options > Keep in Dock.

You can also rearrange items in the Dock—just drag an item to a new location.

Customize the Dock

1. On your Mac, choose Apple menu > System Preferences, then click Dock.
2. Change the options you want.

   For example, you can change how items appear in the Dock, adjust its size and position, or even hide it.

   To learn about the options, click the Help button ? in the pane.

To quickly adjust the Dock's size, place the pointer over the separator line until a double arrow appears, then drag the Dock to make it larger or smaller. Or Control-click the separator and choose an action from the shortcut menu.

You can use keyboard shortcuts to navigate to the Dock. Press Control-F3 (Control-Fn-F3 on a portable Mac) to move to the Dock. Then use the Left Arrow and Right Arrow keys to move from icon to icon. Press Return to open an item.

A red badge on an icon in the Dock indicates you need to take one or more actions in an app or System Preferences. For example, a red badge on the Mail icon in the Dock indicates you have new emails to read.

When you drag a folder to the Dock, you can view it as a folder stack. By default, the Dock comes with a Downloadsstack.

See and organize your files in the Finder on Mac

The Finder is the home base for your Mac. The Finder icon looks like a blue smiling face; click the icon in the Dock to open a Finder window.

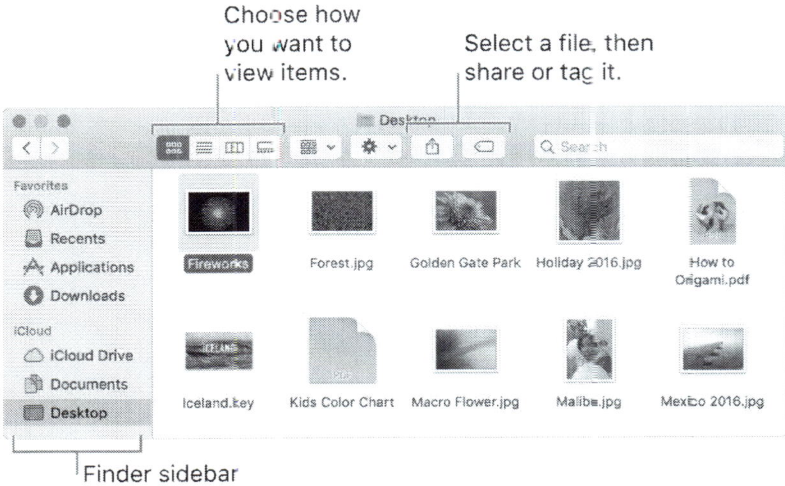

See your stuff

Click items in the Finder sidebar to see your files, apps, downloads, and more. To make the sidebar even more useful, customize it. To make the Finder window even more useful, show the Preview pane.

Or, ask Siri to help you find what you want.

Ask Siri. Say something like:

- "Show me all the files called Expenses"
- "Show me files tagged red"
- "Show me files that are PDFs"

Access everything, everywhere

Use iCloud Drive to automatically store your Desktop and Documents files and folders in iCloud. You can access them on any Mac where you're signed in with the same Apple ID.

Organize with folders or tags

If you like organizing your files in folders, you can do that. It's easy to create new foldersin your Documents folder, on the desktop, or in iCloud Drive.

You can also tag files and folders with helpful keywords to make them easier to find.

Keep your messy desktop clean

Stacks helps you keep files organized in tidy groups on the desktop. You can group stacksby kind, date, or tags. When you group by kind, all your images go in one stack, presentations in another, and so on. Any new files you add go immediately to the correct stack—helping you keep everything in order automatically.

Choose your view

You can choose how you view the items in Finder windows. For example, you don't have to view your items in a list—Gallery view lets you flip through your files and folders visually.

Send it with Airdrop

You can send a file to a nearby Mac, iPhone, or iPad right from the Finder. Click Airdrop in the sidebar to get started. See Use Airdrop to send files to devices near you.

You can also select a file in the Finder, then click the Share button (or use the Touch Bar) to share itusing Mail, Airdrop, Messages, Notes, and more.

Sync information between your Mac and other devices

You can connect your iPhone, iPad, or iPod touch to your Mac to transfer and update items between devices.

For example, when you add a movie to your Mac, you can sync with your iPhone and watch the movie on both devices.

You can sync items including music, movies, TV shows, podcasts, books, and more.

Use keyboard shortcuts to quickly get things done

You can use keyboard shortcuts to quickly perform common actions.

Use the Touch Bar on Mac

If your Mac has a Touch Bar, you can use familiar gestures—like tap, swipe, or slide—directly on the Touch Bar to adjust settings, use Siri, access function keys, and do tasks in different apps.

The Touch Bar includes Touch ID, which lets you unlock your Mac and some password-protected items, use Apple Pay to make purchases on the web, and make purchases from the iTunes Store, the App Store, and Apple Books.

Touch Bar basics

The Control Strip, at the right end of the Touch Bar, lets you adjust common settings—like brightness and volume—and ask Siri. You can expand it to access additional settings and features. The other buttons available in the Touch Bar depend on the app you're using or the task you're doing.

- *Change the brightness or volume, or ask Siri:* Tap the buttons in the Control Strip. For brightness and volume, you can also quickly flick left or right on the buttons.

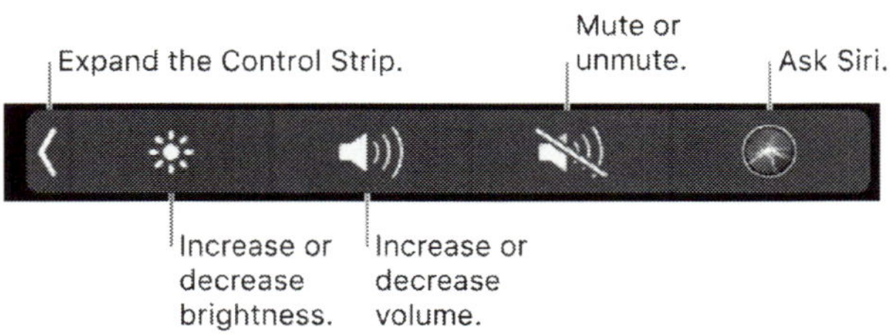

- *Expand the Control Strip:* Tap ‹, or press the FN key on the keyboard (if you customized the Touch Bar in Keyboard preferences to expand the Control Strip).

Tap the buttons in the expanded Control Strip to access additional settings and macOS features like Mission Control and Launchpad, or to control video or music playback. For some settings—such as display brightness—you can touch and hold the button to change the setting.

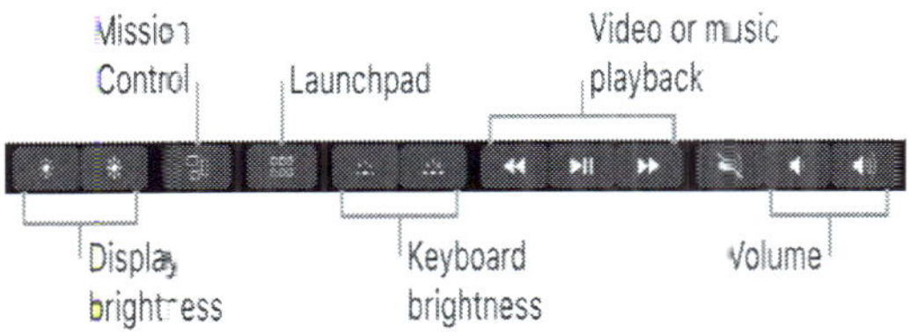

- To collapse the Control Strip, tap  .
- Use *other buttons:* Tap buttons to quickly do tasks in the app you're using. Each app is different—try it out to see what you can do. For example, here's how the Touch Bar looks when you select a file in the Finder:

And here's how it looks when you view a picture in the Photos app:

- To add buttons to the Touch Bar in some apps, ☐

  Add *emoji to your text:* Tap , then tap the emoji you want to use.

Typing suggestions

When you're typing text on your Mac, the Touch Bar can show words or phrases you might want to use next (called *typing suggestions*), to help you save time.

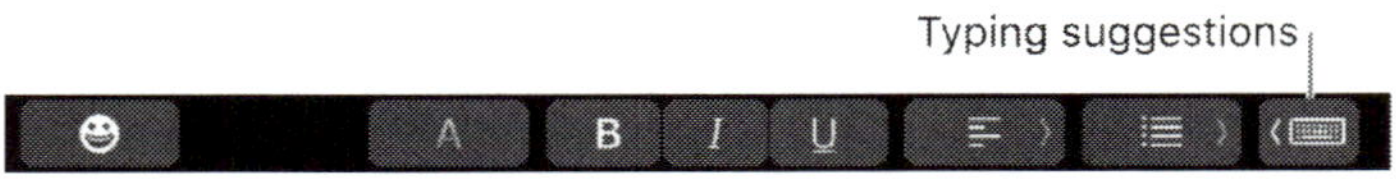

Use typing suggestions: Tap a word, phrase, or emoji. Spelling corrections are shown in blue.

- *Hide typing suggestions:* Tap in the Touch Bar.

If you don't see in the Touch Bar, choose View > Customize Touch Bar, then select "Show typing suggestions." Or choose Apple menu > System Preferences, click Keyboard, click Text, then select "Touch Bar typing suggestions."

Colors

In apps where you can change the color of text or objects, you can use the Touch Bar to select a color, shade, or mode (such as RGB or HSB).

Select a color: Touch and hold A, then slide your finger to a color.

☐ Select *a shade:* Tap A, touch and hold a color, then slide your finger to a shade.

☐ Select *a mode or custom color:* Tap A, tap the color list on the left, then tap a color mode, such as RGB. To use a custom color you saved, tap Swatches.

Use the sliders for a mode to change values, such as hue or saturation. To save your changes to Swatches, tap the color (a + appears), then tap it again (a checkmark appears).

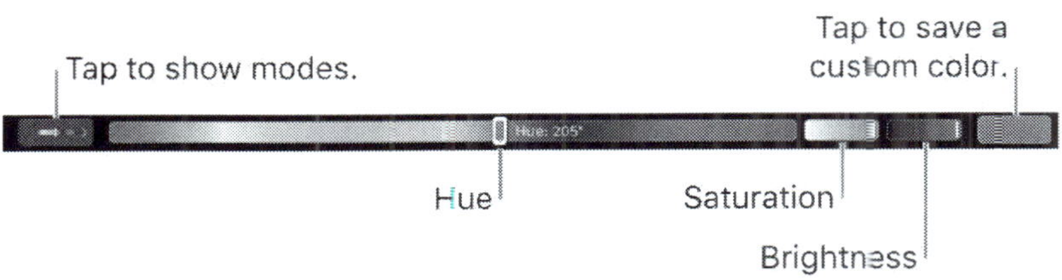

Hide colors or the color values: Tap  in the Touch Bar.

Function keys

Many macOS keyboard shortcuts use function keys (F1 through F12). For example, you can use F11 to show the desktop.

1. Press and hold the FN key on the keyboard to show the function keys in the Touch Bar.

   Make sure you customize the Touch Bar in Keyboard preferences so the FN key shows function keys.

☐ Tap a function key.

If a keyboard shortcut includes a modifier, such as Option or Command, press and hold the FN key with the modifier key. For example, to use Control-F3 to move to the Dock, press and hold the FN and Control keys together, then tap F3 in the Touch Bar.

Use Touch ID on Mac

If your Mac has Touch ID, you can use it to unlock your Mac, authorize purchases from the iTunes Store, the App Store, and Apple Books, and make purchases on the web using Apple Pay. You can also use Touch ID to sign into some third-party apps.

Touch ID is located at the top-right corner of the keyboard, next to the Touch Bar or row of function keys, depending on the model of your Mac.

Set up Touch ID

1. On your Mac, choose Apple menu > System Preferences, then click Touch ID.
2. Click "Add a fingerprint," enter your password, then follow the onscreen instructions.

   You can add up to three fingerprints to your user account (your Mac can store up to five fingerprints total).
3. Click the checkboxes to select how you want to use Touch ID:
   - *Unlocking your Mac:* Use Touch ID to unlock this Mac when you wake it from sleep.

- *Apple Pay:* Use Touch ID to complete purchases you make on this Mac using Apple Pay.
- *ITunes Store, App Store & Apple Books:* Use Touch ID to complete purchases you make on this Mac from the Apple online stores.
- *Password AutoFill:* Use Touch ID to automatically fill in user names and passwords and to automatically fill in credit card information when requested while using Safari and other apps.

Rename or delete fingerprints

1. On your Mac, choose Apple menu > System Preferences, then click Touch ID.
2. Do any of the following:
    - *Rename a fingerprint:* Click the text below a fingerprint, then enter a name.
    - *Delete a fingerprint:* Click a fingerprint, enter your password, and then click Delete.

Use Touch ID to unlock your Mac, log in, or switch users

To use Touch ID for these tasks, you must have logged in to your Mac already by entering your password.

- *Unlock your Mac and some password-protected items:* When you wake your Mac from sleep, or open a password-protected item, just place your finger on Touch ID when asked.
- *Log in from the login window:* Click your name in the login window, then place your finger on Touch ID.

  Only user accounts that have passwords can be unlocked with Touch ID. Share-only users and guest accounts cannot use Touch ID.
- *Switch users:* Click the fast user switching menu in the menu bar, choose a different user, and then place your finger on Touch ID.

  To use Touch ID to switch to another user, you need to have set up fast user switching, and the user you switch to must have logged in to the Mac already by entering a password.

Use Touch ID to purchase items

1. Log in to your Mac by entering your password.
2. Purchase items using Apple Pay or from one of the online Apple stores.
3. Place your finger on Touch ID when asked.

If you have problems with Touch ID

- *If Touch ID doesn't recognize your fingerprint:* Make sure your finger is clean and dry, then try again. Moisture, lotions, cuts, or dry skin can affect fingerprint recognition.
- *If you still have to enter your password:* Sometimes you'll need to enter your password to continue using Touch ID. For example, users must re-enter their password every 48 hours and after five incorrect fingerprint attempts.

Note: For added security, only logged-in users can access their own Touch ID information; an administrator cannot change another user's Touch ID preferences or fingerprints.

Connect your Mac to the internet

These days it's easy to connect to the internet from your Mac, whether you're at home, at work, or on the go. Two common ways to get online are by using a Wi-Fi (wireless) or Ethernet (wired) connection. If neither is available, you may be able to use an Instant Hotspot.

Use Wi-Fi

When a Wi-Fi network is available to your Mac, the Wi-Fi icon is shown in the menu bar at the top of the screen. Click the icon, then choose a network to join. If you see a lock icon next to the network name, the network is protected by a password—you'll need to enter the password before you can use that Wi-Fi network.

Use Ethernet

You can use Ethernet either through an Ethernet network or through a DSL or cable modem. If Ethernet is available, connect an Ethernet cable to the Ethernet port on your Mac, identified by this symbol <•••>. If your Mac doesn't include a built-in Ethernet port, you can use an adapter to connect the Ethernet cable to the USB or Thunderbolt port on your computer.

Use Instant Hotspot

If you don't have access to a Wi-Fi or Ethernet connection, you may be able to use your Mac and Instant Hotspot to connect to the internet using the personal hotspot on your iPhone or iPad, as long as they're within range of each other.

At home, at work, or on the go

When you're at home: Your ISP may offer a Wi-Fi or Ethernet internet connection. Check with your ISP if you're not sure which type of access you have.

When you're at work: You may have a Wi-Fi or Ethernet network connection available. Check with your company's IT department or network administrator for details about how to connect to your work network, and usage policies.

When you're on the go: You can use Wi-Fi hotspots (wireless networks that are open to the public) or Instant Hotspot on your Mac (if your Mac and your phone carrier support it). Keep in mind that some Wi-Fi hotspots require that you enter a password, agree to terms of service, or pay a fee to use it.

Keep your Mac up to date

Periodically, Apple releases updates to your macOS software (which can include updates to apps that come with your Mac and important security updates).

If you receive a notification that software updates are available, you can choose when to install the updates, or choose to be reminded the next day. You can also check for macOS updates manually in the Software Update pane of System Preferences.

To check for updates to software you've downloaded from the App Store, open the App Store.

Check for Mac updates manually

To install updates manually on your Mac, do one of the following:

- To download macOS software updates, choose Apple menu > System Preferences, then click Software Update.

Tip: You can also choose Apple menu > About This Mac, then click Software Update.

- To update software downloaded from the App Store, choose Apple menu > App Store, then click Updates.

Set your Mac to check for software updates automatically

1. On your Mac, choose Apple menu > System Preferences, then click Software Update.
2. To automatically install macOS updates, select "Automatically keep my Mac up to date."
3. To set advanced update options, click Advanced, then do any of the following:
    - To have your Mac check for updates automatically, select "Check for updates."
    - To have your Mac download updates without asking, select "Download new updates when available."
    - To have your Mac install macOS updates automatically, select "Install macOS updates."

- To have your Mac install app updates from the App Store automatically, select "Install app updates from the App Store."
- To have your Mac install system files and security updates automatically, select "Install system data files and security updates."

4. Click OK.

To receive the latest updates automatically, it's recommended that you select "Check for updates," "Download new updates when available," and "Install system data files and security updates."

Note: MacBook, MacBook Pro, and MacBook Air must have the power adapter plugged in to automatically download updates.

Use built-in help on your Mac

The Finder and most apps on your Mac have a Help menu in the menu bar so you can easily get information about macOS, your Mac, and the apps you use.

Tip: If you see a Help button  in the user interface—for example, in a preference pane or dialog—click it to get information about options and actions related to the pane or dialog you see on the screen.

Use the Help menu

In the Finder or an app on your Mac, choose Help in the menu bar, then do one of the following.

- *Open the macOS User Guide or the User Guide for an app:* Choose macOS Help or [*App*] Help (such as Mail Help).
- *Search for a menu item or help topics:* Start entering a search term in the search field. The Help menu lists menu items and help topics related to the term.

  To see where a menu item is located, move the pointer over it in the list. To open a help topic in the help window, choose it in the list. Or choose Show All Help Topics.

Use the help window

When you use the macOS User Guide or the User Guide for an app, you can easily browse more topics, search the guide, and more.

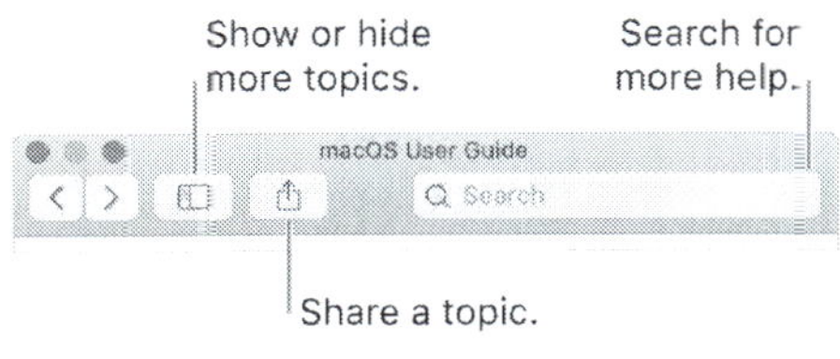

In a user guide on your Mac, do any of the following:

- *Search for help topics:* Enter a search term in the search field, then choose a suggestion or press Return.

- *Show or hide more topics:* Click the Table of Contents button .
- *Show the previous or next topic that you browsed:* Click the Previous and Next buttons.
- *See a list of recently viewed topics:* Click and hold the Back or Forward button until a list appears, then choose the topic you want.
- *Make text bigger or smaller:* Press Command-Plus (+) or Command-Minus (–).
- *Resize the window:* Drag the right or bottom edge of the window.
- *Find words within the current topic:* Press Command-F, then enter the word you want to find.
- *Print or share a topic:* Click the Share button in the help window, then choose an option.

If you can't find what you're looking for when you search help, try entering different words or more or fewer words in the help window search field.

Chapter 2

Maximizing the Apps

Apps included on your Mac

Your Mac comes with a wide range of apps already installed so you can have fun, work, connect with friends, get organized, buy things, and more. To open apps, click their icons in the Dock or click the Launchpad icon in the Dock, then use Launchpad to open apps.

Tip: Every app that comes with your Mac includes help so you can become a pro using it. Just choose Help in the menu bar while using the app.

You can change the look of the menu bar, desktop picture, Dock, and built-in apps appearance in System Preferences.

During downtime, or if you reach the time limit set for apps in Screen Time preferences, app icons are dimmed and an hourglass icon is shown.

Use Launchpad to view and open apps on Mac

Launchpad on your Mac is a central location where you can see and open apps that are on your Mac.

Open and close Launchpad

- *Open Launchpad:* Click its icon in the Dock(or use the Control Strip).

- *Close Launchpad without opening an app:* Click anywhere (except on an app) or press Esc.

Find and open apps in Launchpad

- *Find an app:* Type its name in the search field at the top of Launchpad. Or look on another page in Launchpad—swipe left or right on the trackpad or press Command-Left Arrow or Command-Right Arrow.
- *Open an app:* Click it.

During downtime, or if you reach the time limit set for apps in Screen Time preferences, app icons are dimmed and an hourglass icon is shown.

Organize apps in Launchpad

- *Move an app on a page:* Drag an app to a new location on the same page.
- *Move an app to another page:* Drag the app to the edge of the screen, then release it when the page you want appears.
- *Create an app folder:* Drag an app over another app. To add another app, drag it over the folder. To remove an app, drag it out of the folder.

  Tip: Don't like the name of a folder? Click the folder to open it, click its name, and then type a new name.

Add apps to Launchpad

Apps that you download from the App Store automatically appear in Launchpad.

Add an app that you didn't download from the App Store: Drag the app to the Applications folder in the Finderon your Mac. The app is then shown in Launchpad.

Remove apps from Launchpad

1. In Launchpad, click and hold an app until all the apps begin to jiggle.

2. Click the app's Delete button .

   If you don't see a Delete button, the app can't be removed from Launchpad.

You can drag an item from Launchpad to add it to the Dock. The app is in the Dock and in Launchpad.

Manage windows on Mac

When you open an app or the Finder on your Mac, a window opens on the desktop. Only one app at a time is active; the name of the app (in bold) and the app menus are shown in the menu bar.

Some apps, such as Safari or Mail, let you open multiple windows or different types of windows at the same time. MacOS provides several ways to manage open apps and windows.

Move, align, and merge windows

On your Mac, do any of the following:

- *Move a window:* Drag the window by its title bar to where you want it. Some windows can't be moved.
- *Align windows:* Drag a window close to another one—as the window nears the other one, it aligns without overlapping. You can position multiple windows adjacent to each other.

  To make adjacent windows the same size, drag the edge you want to resize—as it nears the edge of the adjacent window, it aligns with the edge and stops

  Drag the edge until it stops aligned with the edge of the adjacent window.
- Merge *an app's windows into one tabbed window:* In the app, choose Window > Merge All Windows.

To make a tab a separate window again, select the tab, then choose Window > Move Tab to New Window, or just drag the tab out of the window.

Maximize or minimize windows

On your Mac, do any of the following in a window:

- *Maximize a window:* Press and hold the Option key while you click the green maximize button  in the top-left corner of an app window. To return to the previous window size, Option-click the button again.

You can also double-click an app's title bar to maximize the window (as long as the option to do so is set to "zoom" in Dock preferences).

- *Minimize a window:* Click the yellow minimize button  in the top-left corner of the window, or press Command-M.

  You can set an option in Dock preferences to have a window minimize when you double-click its title bar.

Most windows can be manually resized. Drag the window's edge (top, bottom, or sides) or double-click an edge to expand that side of the window.

Quickly switch between app windows

On your Mac, do any of the following:

- *Switch to the previous app:* Press Command-Tab.
- *Scroll through all open apps:* Press and hold the Command key, press the Tab key, then press the Left or Right arrow key until you get to the app you want. Release the Command key.

  If you change your mind while scrolling through the apps and don't want to switch apps, press Esc

(Escape) or the Period key, then release the Command key.

Close a window

- In a window on your Mac, click the red close button in the top-left corner of the window, or press Command-W.

If an app can have multiple windows open, such as Safari or Mail, closing a window does not close or quit the app. To quit these apps, click the app's name in the menu bar, then choose Quit [*App*]. You can hide or quit the active app by pressing Command-H or Command-Q.

You can use Mission Controlto quickly arrange open windows and spaces in a single layer to easily spot the one you need.

Use apps in full screen on Mac

On your Mac, move the pointer to the green button in the top-left corner of the window, then choose Enter Full Screen from the menu that appears or click the button .

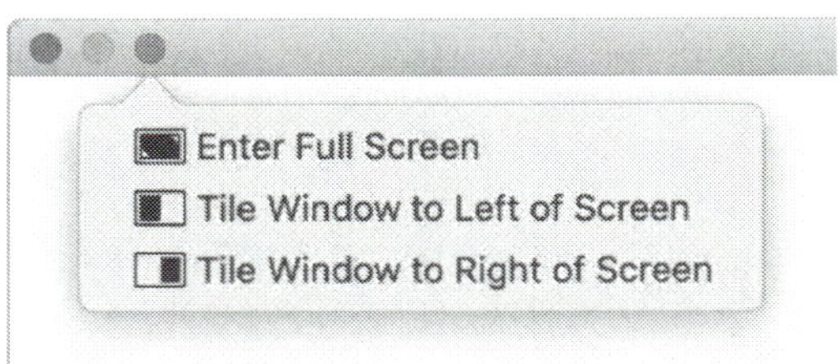

- In full screen, do any of the following:
- *Show or hide the menu bar:* Move the pointer to or away from the top of the screen.
- *Show or hide the Dock:* Move the pointer to or away from the Dock's location.
- *Move between other apps in full screen:* Swipe left or right on the trackpad.
- To stop using the app full screen, move the pointer to the green button again, then choose Exit Full Screen from the menu that appears or click the button .

To work in a bigger window without going full screen, maximize (or zoom) the window. Move the pointer to the green button in the top-left corner of the window, press and hold the Option key, then choose Zoom from the menu that appears or click the button . The window expands, but the menu bar and the Dock remain visible. To return to the previous window size, press and hold the Option key, then click the green button again.

You can also double-click an app's title bar to maximize the window. If the app minimizes into the Dock instead, change the title bar setting in Dock preferences.

If you're using an app full screen, you can quickly choose another app to use in Split View. Press Control-Up Arrow (or swipe up with three or four fingers) to enter Mission Control, then drag a window from Mission Control onto the thumbnail of the full-screen app in the Spaces bar. You can also drag one app thumbnail onto another in the Spaces bar.

Use apps in Split View on Mac

Many apps on your Mac support Split View mode, where you can work in two apps side by side at the same time.

On your Mac, move the pointer to the green button in the top-left corner of the window, then choose Tile Window to Left of Screen or Tile Window to Right of Screen from the menu that appears.

1. On the other side of the screen, click the second app you want to work with.
2. In Split View, do any of the following:
    - *Make one side bigger:* Move the pointer over the separator bar located in the middle, then drag it left or right. To return to the original sizes, double-click the separator bar.
    - *Change sides:* Use a window's toolbar to drag the window to the other side. If you don't see a

toolbar, click the window, then move the pointer to the top of the screen.

- *Show or hide the menu bar:* Move the pointer to or away from the top of the screen.
- *Show or hide the Dock:* Move the pointer to or away from the Dock's location.

3. To stop using an app in Split View, click its window, show the menu bar, move the pointer to the green button in the top-left corner of the window, then choose Exit Full Screen from the menu that appears or click the button .

   The remaining app expands to full screen and can be accessed in the Spaces bar. To stop using the app full screen, move the pointer over its thumbnail in the Spaces bar, then click the Exit button  that appears in the top-left corner of the thumbnail.

If you're using an app full screen, you can quickly choose another app to work with in Split View. Press Control-Up Arrow (or swipe up with three or four fingers) to enter Mission Control, then drag a window from Mission Control onto the thumbnail of the full-screen app in the Spaces bar. You can also drag one app thumbnail onto another in the Spaces bar.

Find, buy, and download apps in the App Store on Mac

To find the perfect app, search for it or browse the App Store. Once you find the app you want, you can purchase it using your Apple ID, or you can redeem a download code or a gift card.

To change your settings for downloads and purchases, choose Apple Menu > System Preferences > Apple ID, click Media & Purchases in the sidebar, then choose your options.

Find and buy apps

1. In the App Store on your Mac, do any of the following:
   - *Search for an app:* Enter one or more words in the search field at the top-left corner of the App Store window, then press Enter.
   - *Browse the App Store:* Click Discover, Create, Work, Play, Develop, or Categories in the sidebar on the left.
2. Click an app's name or icon to get a description and view customer ratings and reviews.
3. To download the app, click the button that shows the price of the app or "Get." Then click the button again to install or buy the app (or use Touch ID).

Change your settings for downloads and purchases

1. In the App Store on your Mac, choose Apple Menu > System Preferences.
2. Click Apple ID.
3. Click Media & Purchases (in the sidebar).
4. Choose your options.

Redeem iTunes gift cards, Apple Music cards, or a download code

- In the App Store on your Mac, click your name in the bottom-left corner (or click Sign In if you're not already), then click Redeem Gift Card in the top-right corner. Enter the download code or the code from your gift card.

  If you have a gift card with a box around the code, you can use the built-in camera on your Mac to redeem the card. After you click Redeem, click Use Camera, then hold the gift card 4 to 7 inches (10 to 18 centimeters) from the camera. Make sure the code area is near the center of the preview area, then hold the card steady until its redeemed.

Purchase in-app content and subscriptions

- Some apps sell extra content, including app upgrades, game content, and subscriptions. To make an in-app purchase, enter your Apple ID(or use Touch ID).

Download apps purchased by other family members

If you're part of a Family Sharing group, you can download eligible apps purchased by other family members.

1. In the App Store on your Mac, click your name in the bottom-left corner, or click Sign In if you're not already.
2. Click the "Purchased by" menu, then choose a family member.
3. Click the iCloud status icon next to an item to download it.

Install and reinstall apps purchased from the App Store on Mac

There are several ways to install and reinstall apps that you purchased with your Apple ID or that came with your new Mac.

Note: In the App Store, all of your purchases are tied to your Apple ID, and can't be transferred to another Apple ID. If you make purchases on your iPhone, iPad, or another Mac, always sign in using the same Apple ID so you can see all of your store purchases on this Mac and download any available updates.

Install apps that you purchased on a different computer

You can install and reinstall any app that you purchased with your Apple ID on other Mac computers.

- In the App Store on your Mac, click your name in the bottom-left corner, or click Sign In if you're not already, then click the redownload button .

Automatically download apps that you purchased on a different computer

1. In the App Store on your Mac, click your name in the bottom-left corner, or click Sign In if you're not already.
2. Choose App Store > Preferences, then select "Automatically download apps purchased on other Mac computers."

Reinstall apps

If you uninstalled or deleted an app that you purchased in the App Store, you can install it again.

- In the App Store on your Mac, click your name in the bottom-left corner, or click Sign In if you're not already, locate the app you want, then click the redownload button .

Manage subscriptions

You can view or change options for subscriptions you purchased in the App Store, the iTunes Store, or Apple News.

1. In the App Store on your Mac, click your name in the bottom-left corner, or click Sign In if you're not already.

   Make sure you sign in with the same Apple ID you used to purchase your subscriptions.

2. Click View Information, sign in again if necessary, and then click Manage (to the right of Subscriptions).
3. Click Edit (if you have more than one subscription), then do any of the following:
   - *Change subscription options:* In the Options list, select a setting, then click done.
   - *Cancel your subscription:* Click Cancel Subscription, confirm the cancellation, then click done.

Reinstall apps that came with your Mac

If an app is damaged or not working, you can try to reinstall it.

- To reinstall an app that came with macOS (for example, Music, Photos, Calendar, Safari, and more), reinstall macOS.

  Reinstalling macOS doesn't erase your information.

  If the apps came on a disc, and don't appear in the App Store, use the disc to reinstall them.

Install and uninstall apps from the internet or disc on Mac

You can download and install apps from the internet or a disc. If you no longer want an app, you can remove it.

Install apps

On your Mac, do any of the following:

- *For apps downloaded from the internet:* In the Downloads folder, double-click the disk image or package file (looks like an open box). If the provided installer doesn't open automatically, open it, then follow the onscreen instructions.

  Note: If you get a warning dialog about installing an app from an unidentified developer, *for apps on a disc:* Insert the disc into the optical drive on your Mac or connected to your Mac.

Uninstall apps

You can remove apps that you downloaded and installed from the internet or from a disc.

1. On your Mac, click the Finder icon  in the Dock, then click Applications in the Finder sidebar.
2. Do one of the following:
    - If an app is in a folder, open the app's folder to check for an Uninstaller. If you see Uninstall [*App*] or [*App*] Uninstaller, double-click it, then follow the onscreen instructions.
    - If an app isn't in a folder or doesn't have an Uninstaller, drag the app from the Applications folder to the Trash (at the end of the Dock).

      WARNING: The app is permanently removed from your Mac the next time you or the Finder empties the Trash. If you have files that you created with the app, you may not be able to open them again. If you decide you want to keep the app, get it back before emptying the Trash—select the app in the Trash, then choose File > Put Back.

Chapter 3

Customize your Mac

Customize your Mac with System Preferences

You can change system settings to customize your Mac. For example, you can change the size and location of the Dock, choose a light or dark appearance, change the desktop picture, and more.

To change System Preferences on your Mac, click the System Preferences icon  in the Dock or choose Apple menu  > System Preferences.

Explore preferences

Options for your Mac are organized into preferences. For example, options you can set for Spotlight are located in Spotlight preferences.

Preferences appear as a grid of icons; the icons shown may vary depending on your Mac and the apps you have installed. Click an icon to open a preference pane and see the options.

By default, preferences are arranged in rows by category. To see them in alphabetical order, choose View > Organize Alphabetically.

Set options

Each preference pane contains options you can set. Most panes include a Help button  to click for more information about the options.

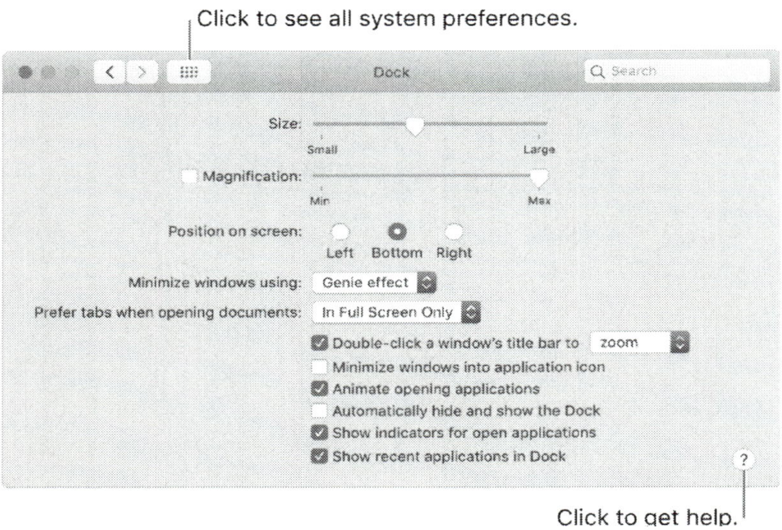

Some panes are locked to protect your Mac, indicated by a closed lock icon at the bottom of the pane, and the options are dimmed. To unlock a pane so you can set options, click the lock icon, and then enter the administrator password for your Mac.

Find options

If you don't know where to find an option in System Preferences, use the search field at the top of the window. Options that match your search text are listed, and the preference panes where they're located are highlighted.

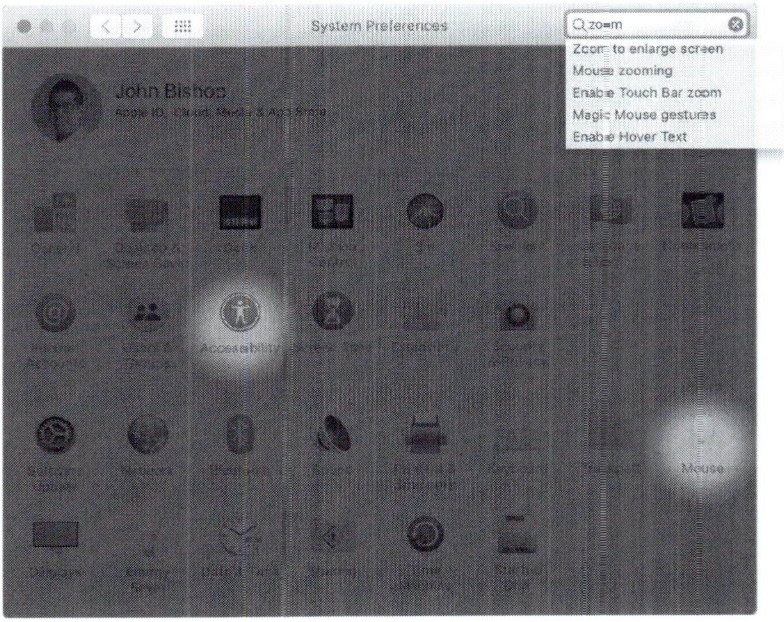

If you see a red badge on the System Preferences icon in the Dock, you need to take one or more actions. For example, if you didn't fully set up iCloud, the badge appears on the icon in the Dock; when you click the icon, the preferences are displayed so you can complete setup.

To change options for an app, such as Mail or Safari, open the app, click the app's name in the menu bar, and then choose Preferences.

Customize the desktop picture on your Mac

You can choose the picture that's displayed on your desktop. Your Mac comes with dozens of desktop pictures to choose from, or you can use your own pictures or choose a solid color.

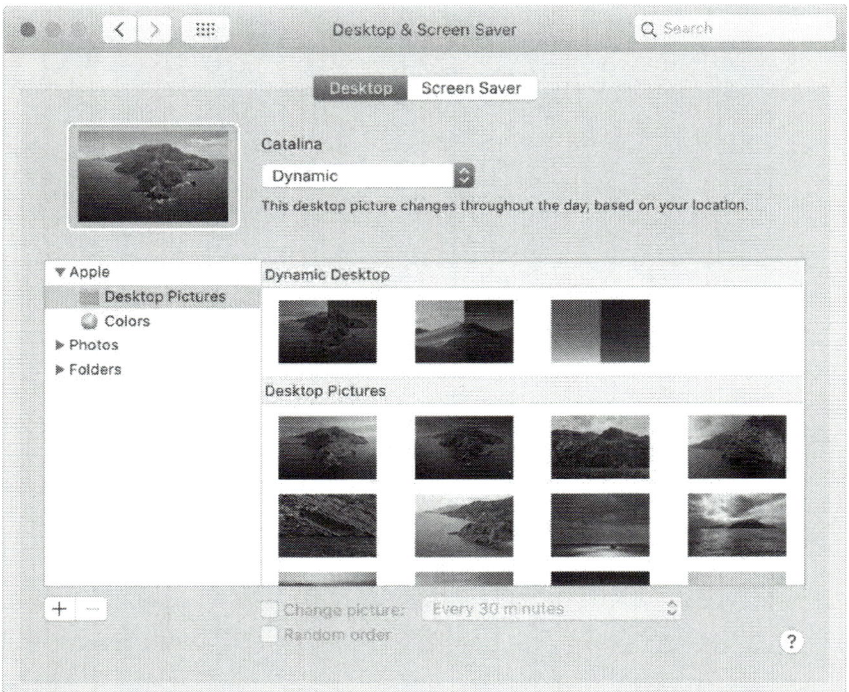

Tip: You can drag an image from your desktop or a folder onto the thumbnail at the top of the pane to use the image as your desktop picture.

1. On your Mac, choose Apple menu > System Preferences, click Desktop & Screen Saver, then click Desktop.

2. On the left, find a picture or color:

   - *Pictures and colors that come with your Mac:* Click the disclosure triangle next to Apple, then select Desktop Pictures or Colors to see thumbnails of available pictures and colors.

     Dynamic desktop pictures can automatically change throughout the course of the day based on your current location. If Location Services is turned off in Privacy preferences, the picture changes based on the time zone specified in Date & Time preferences.

     Some dynamic desktop pictures may also provide still images so the desktop picture doesn't distract from the light or dark appearance. For example, if you chose the dark appearance during macOS setup, the desktop picture is set to a dark still image. To use or stop using a still image (if available), click the pop-up menu, then choose an option.

   - *Your pictures:* Click the disclosure triangle next to Photos (or iPhoto if available). If your pictures are in the Pictures or another folder, click the triangle next to Folders, then select a folder.

To add a folder, click the Add button +, navigate to and select the folder, then click Choose.

If you don't see anything when you select the folder that contains your pictures, they might not have the right file format—JPEG, PICT, TIFF, PNG, or HEIC. To change a picture's format, open it in the Preview app, then save it in the new format. If pictures look fuzzy, try using larger ones, such as 1024 x 768 pixels.

3. On the right, click the picture you want to use.

The desktop immediately changes, so you can see how the picture looks. When you use one of your own pictures, you can choose to have it fill the screen, be centered, or otherwise arranged. It's easy to click around and try different pictures and arrangements until you find the one you like best.

To use all the pictures in a folder, select the "Change picture" checkbox, then choose how often you want the picture to change—for example, every hour. The pictures are shown in the order they appear in the folder, or you can choose to show them in a random order.

To quickly use a picture you have in the Photos app, select the picture in Photos, click the Share button in the Photos toolbar, then choose Set Desktop Picture.

You can use a picture you see on the web as your desktop picture. Control-click the image in the browser window, then select Use Image as Desktop Picture.

Use your internet accounts on Mac

You can use Exchange, Google, Yahoo, and other internet accounts in Mac apps by adding the accounts to your Mac.

You add internet accounts, and manage account settings, in Internet Accounts preferences. You can also add internet accounts from some apps that use them.

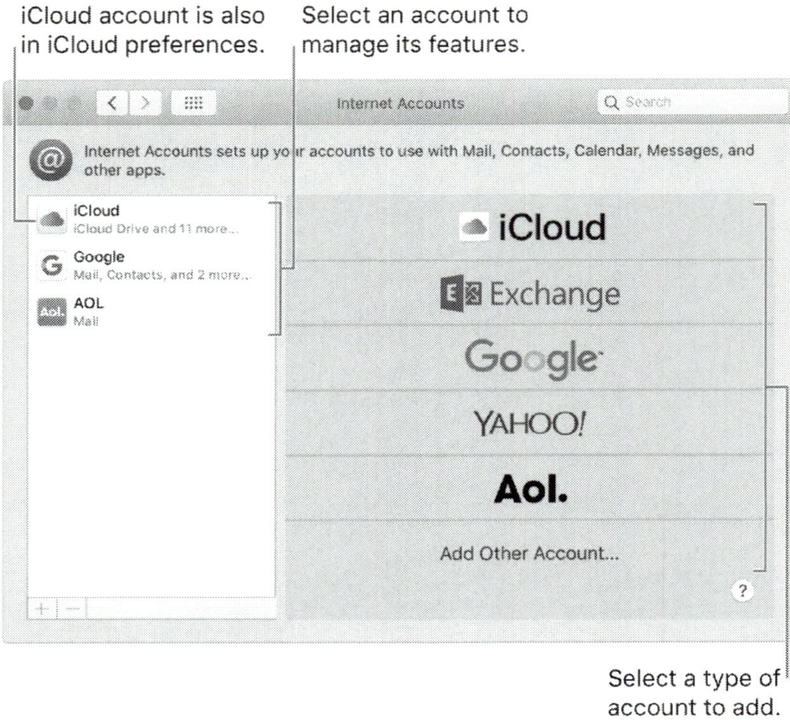

An iCloud account you add using the iCloud preferences in Apple ID preferences also appears in Internet Accounts preferences. You can change its settings in either place.

Add an account from an app

You can add accounts from Mail, Contacts, and Calendar. Accounts you add from the apps appear in Internet Accounts preferences.

1. In an app on your Mac, click the app menu, then choose Add account.

For example, in Mail, choose Mail > Add account.

2. Select the account provider, then follow the onscreen instructions.

   If you want to add an account from a provider that isn't listed, such as a mail or calendar account for your company or school, click Other [*Type of*] Account, click Continue, then enter the requested account settings. If you don't know the account settings, ask the account provider.

Add an account in Internet Accounts preferences

Before you can add an account in Internet Accounts preferences, you must create the account on the provider's website.

1. On your Mac, choose Apple menu > System Preferences, then click Internet Accounts.
2. Click an account provider.

   If you don't yet have an account from a particular provider, such as Yahoo, create one on the provider's website, then add it here.

   If you want to add an account from a provider that isn't listed, such as a mail or calendar account for your company or school, click Add Other Account on the right, click the type of account you want to add, then enter the requested account settings. If you don't know the type of account or the account settings, ask the account provider.

3. Enter your account name, password, and other requested information, then click Set Up.
4. If the account you added has a list of features on the right, select the ones you want to use.

Change account features and details

1. On your Mac, choose Apple menu > System Preferences, then click Internet Accounts.
2. Select an account on the left, then do one of the following:
    - *Turn features on or off:* Select each feature you want to use, and deselect any feature you don't want to use.
    - *Change account details:* For the selected account, click Details on the right. Some accounts show the account name, a description, and other details on the right and don't have a Details button.

Stop using an account

1. On your Mac, choose Apple menu > System Preferences, then click Internet Accounts.
2. Select the account you want to stop using, then do one of the following:
   - *Remove the account and turn off its features:*

     Click the Remove button .

     If your Mac is set up for iCloud Keychainand you remove an account (other than your primary iCloud account), you're asked whether to remove the account from your other Mac computers set up for iCloud Keychain or just turn off all the account features on this Mac.
   - *Turn off a specific feature:* Deselect it.

   Note: Deleting an account or turning off individual features can remove data stored in your apps. The data may be restored if you turn on the feature or add the account again. If you're not sure, ask the account provider.

Set up Screen Time for yourself on Mac

On your Mac, turn on Screen Time to learn how you spend time on your Mac and other devices. When Screen Time is turned on, you can view reports that show app usage, the number of notifications you receive, and how often you use your devices.

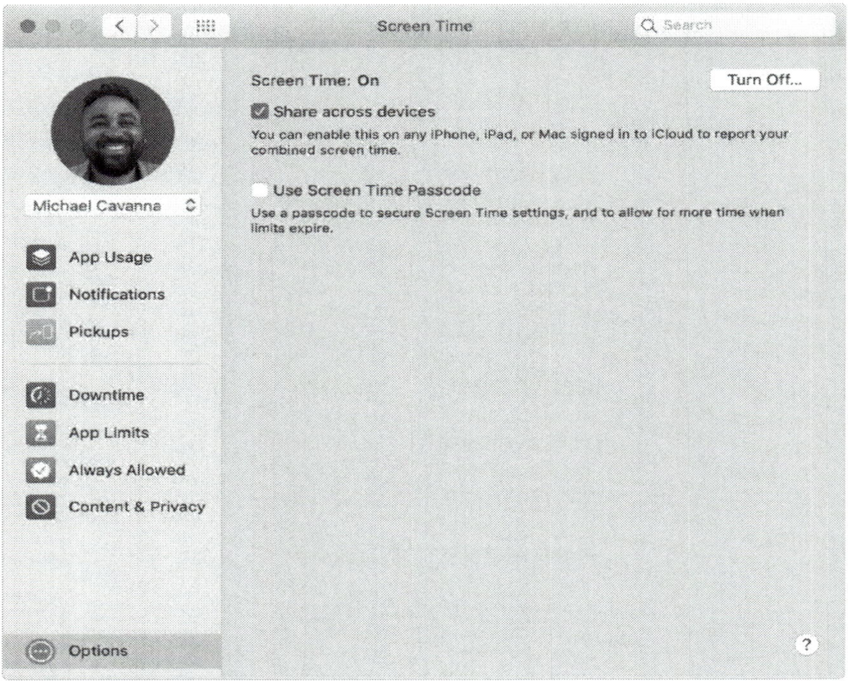

1. On your Mac, choose Apple menu > System Preferences, then click Screen Time.
2. If you're a member of a Family Sharing group, click the pop-up menu in the sidebar, then choose yourself.

   If you aren't using Family Sharing, you won't see a pop-up menu in the sidebar.
3. Click Options in the lower-left corner of the sidebar.

4. Click Turn On in the upper-right corner.
5. Select any of the following options:
    - *Share across devices:* Select this option if you want Screen Time reports to include time spent on other devices signed in with the same Apple ID.

      This option is available only when you're signed in with your Apple ID.
    - *Use Screen Time Passcode:* Select this option to secure Screen Time settings, and to require a passcode to allow additional time when limits expire.
6. If you want to, do any of the following:
    - Click Downtime in the sidebar, then set up a downtime schedule.
    - Click App Limits in the sidebar, then set time limits for apps and websites.
    - Click Always Allowed in the sidebar, then choose apps that can be used at any time.
    - Click Content & Privacy in the sidebar, then set up content & privacy restrictions.

Change the appearance of the desktop

- *Make the desktop less transparent:* Choose Apple menu > System Preferences, click Accessibility, click Display, click Display, and then select "Reduce transparency." The transparent areas of the desktop and app windows become gray.
- *Choose a desktop picture with fewer colors or shapes:* Choose Apple menu > System Preferences, click Desktop & Screen Saver, click Desktop, browse through the picture folders on the left, then select a less busy picture or a solid color on the right.
- *Make borders darker:* Choose Apple menu > System Preferences, click Accessibility, click Display, click Display, then select "Increase contrast." macOS automatically reduces transparency and makes the borders of buttons, boxes, and other items on the screen more visible.
- *Use a dark appearance:* Choose Apple menu > System Preferences, click General, then click the Dark appearance. You can change the accent and highlight colors.

- *Invert colors:* Choose Apple menu > System Preferences, click Accessibility, click Display, click Display, and then select "Invert colors." If you turn on Night Shift, "Invert colors" is automatically disabled.

- *Make colors easier on your eyes at night:* Use NightShift to make the colors on the screen warmer.

- *Differentiate or tone down colors:* Apply color filtersor tint the entire screen.

- *Make the pointer bigger:* Choose Apple menu > System Preferences, click Accessibility, click Display, click Cursor, then drag the Cursor Size slider to the right as far as you need.

  Tip: If you lose track of the pointer on the screen, quickly move your finger on the trackpad or quickly move the mouse—the pointer briefly gets bigger so you can see it. To turn this feature off, choose Apple menu > System Preferences, click Accessibility, click Display, click Cursor, then deselect "Shake mouse pointer to locate."

Make text bigger

- *Increase the text size of emails in Mail:* In Mail, choose Mail > Preferences, click Fonts & Colors, click Select next to "Message font," then select a font size in the Fonts window.

- *Increase the text size of messages in Messages:* In Messages, choose Messages > Preferences, click General, then move the "Text size" slider to the right.
- *Increase the text size in other apps:* In many apps, you can press Command-Plus (+) or Command-Minus (–) to adjust text size. If that doesn't work, check the app's preferences.

Make icons and other items bigger

- *Increase the size of icons and text on the desktop:* Control-click the desktop, choose Show View Options, then move the "Icon size" slider to the right. Click the "Text size" pop-up menu, then choose a text size.
- *Increase the size of icons and text in the Finder:* Select an item in the Finder, then choose View > Show View Options. The view you're usingdetermines how you increase the size.
    - *Icon view:* Move the "Icon size" slider to the right. Click the "Text size" pop-up menu, then choose a text size.
    - *List view:* Select the larger icon size to the right of "Icon size." Click the "Text size" pop-up menu, then choose a text size.

- *Column view:* Click the "Text size" pop-up menu, then choose a text size. You can't choose an icon size.
- *Gallery view:* Select the largest thumbnail size. You can't choose a text size.

- *Increase the size of items in the Finder and Mail sidebars:* Choose Apple menu > System Preferences, click General, click the "Sidebar icon size" pop-up menu, then choose Large.

Use zoom

- *Zoom in on the screen:* Choose Apple menu > System Preferences, click Accessibility, then click Zoom. You can zoom the entire screen or an area of it.
    - When "Use keyboard shortcuts to zoom" is selected, you can zoom in (press Option-Command-Equal sign), zoom out (press Option-Command-Minus sign), or quickly switch between the two settings (press Option-Command-8).
    - When "Use scroll gesture with modifier keys to zoom" is selected, you can zoom in by pressing and holding the Control key (or

another modifier key) and swiping up with two fingers on your trackpad.

- *Zoom in on the item under the pointer:* Choose Apple menu > System Preferences, click Accessibility, click Zoom, and then select Enable Hover Text. *Zoom in on webpages:* In Safari, choose View > Zoom In, or press Command-Plus (+). You can choose Zoom In or press Command-Plus multiple times to continue zooming in. If you want to zoom just the text and not images, choose Zoom Text Only.
- *Zoom in on PDFs, images, and webpages:* If your mouse or trackpad supports it, you can zoom in or out using a simple gesture. Choose Apple menu > System Preferences, click Mouse > Point & Click or Trackpad > Scroll & Zoom, then select Smart zoom. Now to zoom in or out, double-tap on your mouse with one finger or on your trackpad with two fingers.

Use accessibility features on Mac

Accessibility comes standard with a Mac. Whether you have difficulties with vision, hearing, or physical mobility, macOS includes a variety of features to help you work in alternative ways—and make your Mac even easier to use.

Use the built-in screen reader called Voiceover

Voiceover is the built-in screen reader that describes aloud what appears on your screen and speaks the text in documents, webpages, and windows. Using Voiceover, you control your Mac with the keyboard or trackpad gestures. You can also connect a refreshable braille display to use with Voiceover.

- To turn Voiceover on or off, press Command-F5 (or if your Mac has Touch ID, press and hold the Command key, then quickly press Touch ID three times).
- To customize Voiceover using Voiceover Utility, press Control-Option-F8 (when Voiceover is on).
- To learn how to use Voiceover, choose Apple menu > System Preferences, click Accessibility, click Voiceover, and then click Open Voiceover Training.

For help with Voiceover, choose Help > Voiceover Help while Voiceover Utility is open.

Make content on the screen larger

- You can use your mouse or use your trackpad to zoom and make the entire screen larger or just an area of it. If you're using a second display with your Mac, you can choose which display to zoom—or zoom both.

- You can use Hover Text to zoom whatever is under the pointer—text, fields, menu items, buttons, and more—in high resolution in a separate window.

Reduce motion on the screen

If motion on the screen of your Mac is problematic, you can set an option to reduce motion when using certain features, such as Spaces, Notification Center, or the Dock.

1. Choose Apple menu > System Preferences, click Accessibility, click Display, and then click Display.
2. Select Reduce motion.

Use a physical keyboard or an onscreen keyboard

Set options that make it easier to press keys on a physical keyboard, or bypass a physical keyboard altogether and use the onscreen Accessibility Keyboard instead.

1. Choose Apple menu > System Preferences, click Accessibility, then click Keyboard.
2. Do any of the following:
    - Click Hardware, then turn on Sticky Keys and Slow Keys.
    - Click Accessibility Keyboard, then turn on the Accessibility Keyboard.

You can easily check which accessibility features are on, right from the menu bar: select the checkbox at the bottom of Accessibility preferences to show accessibility status in the menu bar.

You can use the Accessibility Options shortcut panel to quickly turn some options on or off. To select the options that are included in the panel, choose Apple menu > System Preferences, click Accessibility, then click Shortcut.

In some apps, you can have your Mac speak text by choosing Edit > Speech > Start Speaking. This functionality might not be available for all languages.

Change people's pictures in apps on Mac

You can add or change your picture shown in the login window and in various apps on your Mac, and choose pictures to use for your friends, family, and other contacts.

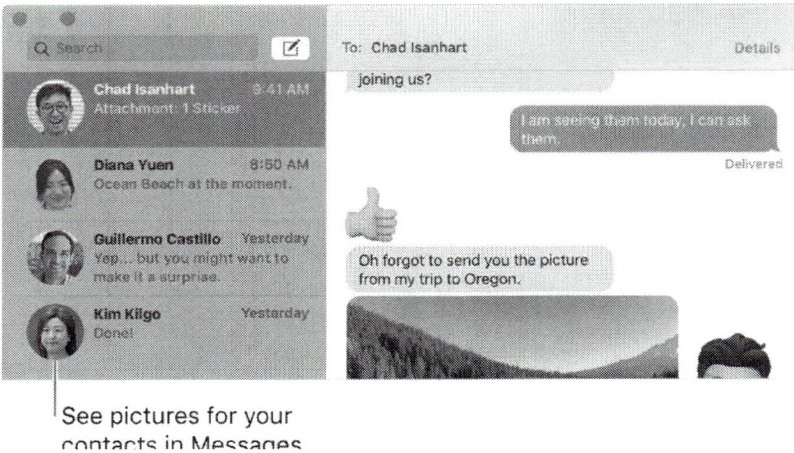

Your user picture

Change the picture that appears next to your name or another user's name in the login window.

Your picture in Messages

Other people see the picture they have stored for you in their Contacts app, and you see the picture you have stored for them in your Contacts. If a picture isn't available, a monogram is shown.

Your picture in Mail

Mail can show a picture for you and for people who email you, depending on the pictures that are available in the Contacts app. The pictures are shown only to you; they aren't included in your emails.

Pictures in Contacts

Include your picture in your contact card. You can also use pictures of people in their contact cards (the pictures may appear in other apps). Your contacts don't see the pictures you choose—only you do.

Set up users, guests, and groups on Mac

If your Mac has multiple users, you should set up an account for each person so each can personalize settings and options without affecting the others. You can let occasional users log in as guests without access to other users' files or settings. You can also create groups. You must be an administratorof your Mac to perform these tasks.

Add a user

1. On your Mac, choose Apple menu > System Preferences, then click Users & Groups.
2. Click the lock icon to unlock it.
3. Enter an administrator name and password.
4. Click the Add button + below the list of users.
5. Click the New Account pop-up menu, then choose a type of user.
   - *Administrator:* An administrator can add and manage other users, install apps, and change settings. The new user you create when you

first set up your Mac is an administrator. Your Mac can have multiple administrators. You can create new ones, and convert standard users to administrators. Don't set up automatic login for an administrator. If you do, someone could simply restart your Mac and gain access with administrator privileges. To keep your Mac secure, don't share administrator names and passwords.

- *Standard:* Standard users are set up by an administrator. Standard users can install apps and change their own settings, but can't add other users or change other users' settings.
- *Sharing Only:* Sharing-only users can access shared files remotely, but can't log in to or change settings on the computer. To give the user permission to access your shared files or screen, you may need to change settings in the File Sharing, Screen Sharing, or Remote Management pane of sharing preferences. See Set up file sharing and Share the screen of another Mac.

For more information about the options for each type of user, click the Help button in the lower-left corner of the dialog.

6. Enter a full name for the new user. An account name is generated automatically. To use a different account name, enter it now—you can't change it later.
7. Enter a password for the user, then enter it again to verify. Enter a password hint to help the user remember their password.
8. Click Create User.
9. Depending on the type of user you create, you can also do any of the following:
   - For an administrator, select "Allow user to administer this computer."
   - Use Sharing preferences to specify whether the user can share your files and share your screen.

For information about Apple's privacy policy,

If your Mac has Touch ID, a new user can add a fingerprint after logging in to the Mac. The user can then use Touch ID to unlock the Mac and password-protected items, and purchase items from the iTunes Store, App Store, and Apple Books using their Apple ID.

Create a group

A group allows multiple users to have the same access privileges. For example, you can grant a group specific access privileges for a folder or a file, and all members of the group have access. You can also assign a group specific access privileges for each of your shared folders.

1. On your Mac, choose Apple menu > System Preferences, then click Users & Groups.
2. Click the lock icon to unlock it.
3. Enter an administratorname and password.
4. Click the Add button below the list of users.
5. Click the New Account pop-up menu, then choose Group.
6. Give the group a name, then click Create Group.
7. Select each user and group you want to add to the new group.

Use Sharing preferences to specify whether the group members can share your filesand share your screen.

Convert a standard user to an administrator

1. On your Mac, choose Apple menu > System Preferences, then click Users & Groups.

2. Click the lock icon to unlock it.
3. Enter an administrator name and password.
4. Select a standard user or managed user in the list of users, then select "Allow user to administer this computer."

Let occasional users log in as guests

You can let other people use your Mac temporarily as guest users without adding them as individual users.

- Guests don't need a password to log in.
- Guests can't change user or computer settings.
- Guests can't log in remotely when remote login is turned on in Sharing preferences.

Files created by a guest are stored in a temporary folder, but that folder and its contents are deleted when the guest logs out.

Guest access works with the Find My app to help you find your Mac if you lose it. You can locate your Mac if someone finds it, logs in as a guest, and then uses Safari to access the internet.

Note: If File Vault is turned on, guests can access Safari, but can't access your encrypted disk or create files.

1. On your Mac, choose Apple menu > System Preferences, then click Users & Groups.
2. Click the lock icon to unlock it.
3. Enter an administrator name and password.
4. Select Guest User in the list of users.
5. Select "Allow guests to log in to this computer."
6. If you like, select "Limit Adult Websites" to prevent the guest from accessing adult websites.
7. To let guests use your shared folders from another computer on the network, select "Allow guest users to connect to shared folders."

Customize the login experience

If you are an administrator, you can specify how the login window looks to all the other users.

1. On your Mac, choose Apple menu > System Preferences, click Users & Groups, then click Login Options.
2. Click the lock icon to unlock it.
3. Enter an administrator name and password.
4. Click the "Automatic login" pop-up menu, then choose a user, or choose off.

If you choose a user, then whenever the Mac starts up, that user is automatically logged in. If you choose off, then at startup the Mac opens a login window showing all the users. Automatic login takes effect the next time you restart the Mac.

Note: Automatic login allows anyone to access your Mac simply by restarting it. If automatic login is enabled, make sure your Mac doesn't automatically log in an administrator. When File Vault is turned on, automatic login is disabled.

5. Select the options you want. If you have any questions, click the Help button for detailed information.

To permit new users to access your shared files or screen, you may need to change settings in the File Sharing, Screen Sharing, or Remote Management pane of sharing preferences. See Set up file sharing and Share the screen of another Mac.

To open Sharing preferences, choose Apple menu > System Preferences, then click Sharing.

Run Windows on your Mac

Use Boot Camp to install and use Windows on your Mac.

Boot Camp Assistant helps you set up a Windows partition on your computer's hard disk and then start the installation of your Windows software.

After installing Windows and the Boot Camp drivers, you can start up your Mac in either Windows or macOS.

Chapter 4

Work with Files and Folders

Create and work with documents on Mac

You can use macOS apps—such as Pages or Text Edit—or apps from the Mac App Store to create reports, essays, spreadsheets, financial charts, presentations, slideshows, and more.

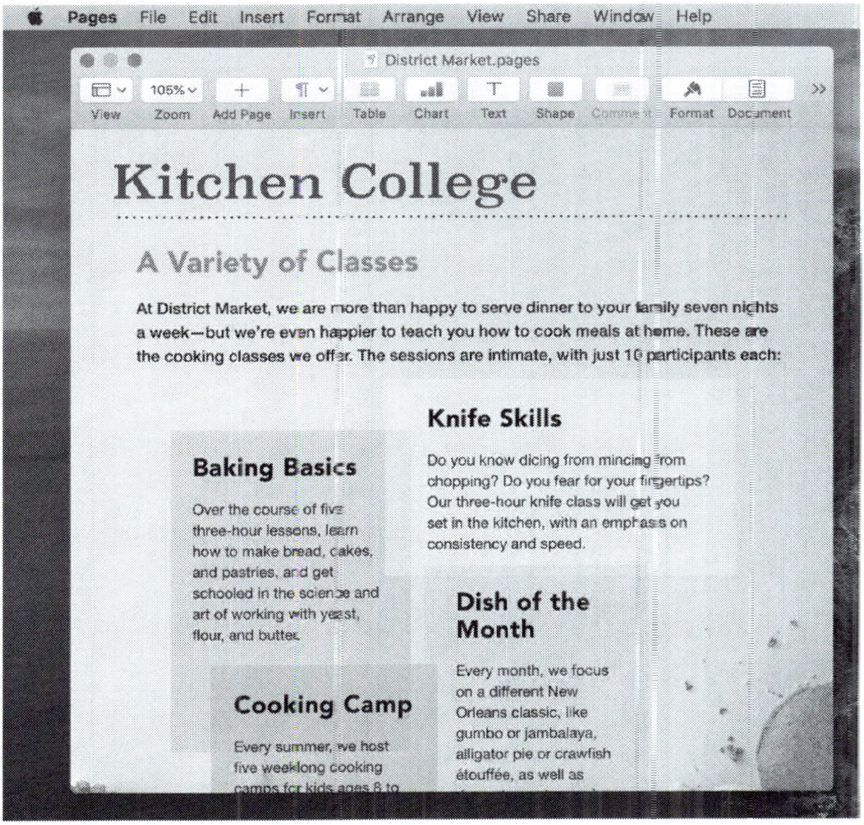

Create documents

1. On your Mac, open an app that lets you create documents.

   For example, open Text Edit to create a plain text, rich text, or HTML document.

2. Click New Document in the Open dialog, or choose File > New.

Many Mac computers come with these Apple apps that you can use to create spreadsheets, presentations, reports, and more.

- *Pages:* Create letters, reports, flyers, posters, and more. Pages includes many templates that make it easy to create beautiful documents.
- *Numbers:* Create spreadsheets to organize and present your data. Start with a template, then modify it however you like—add formulas, charts, images, and more.
- *Keynote:* Create compelling presentations with images, media, charts, slide animations, and more.

If you don't have Pages, Numbers, or Keynote on your Mac, you can get them from the App Store.

They're also available for your iOS and iPadOS devices (from the App Store) and on iCloud.com.

Format documents

There are several ways to format and work with text in documents on your Mac:

- *Change fonts and styles:* In a document, choose Format > Show Fonts or Format > Font > Show Fonts, or Format > Style.
- *Change colors:* In a document, choose Format > Show Colors, or Format > Font > Show Colors. *Enter different types of characters:* You can enter characters with accent marks or diacritic marks.
- *Check spelling:* In most apps, spelling is checked while you type, and mistakes are automatically corrected. You can turn off these features or use other options.

An app may provide additional ways to format and work with text, and with images and objects. To learn more about an app, choose Help in the menu bar while working in the app.

Save documents

Many apps on your Mac save your documents automatically (a feature known as *Auto Save*) while you work. You can save a document at any time.

- *Save a document:* In a document, choose File > Save, enter a name, choose where to save the document (to see more locations, click the down arrow button), then click Save.

When you save your document, you can add tags to help you find it later. You may be able to save your document in iCloud Drive so it's available on your computers and iOS and iPadOS devices set up with iCloud Drive.

- *Save a document with another name:* In a document, choose File > Save As, then enter a new name. If you don't see Save As, press and hold the Option key, then open the File menu again.
- *Save a document as a copy:* In a document, choose File > Duplicate or File > Save As.

You can also save a document as a PDF and combine multiple files into a single PDF.

Find documents

There are several ways to find documents on your Mac:

- *Use Spotlight:* Click the Spotlight icon in the menu bar, then enter the name of your document. You can also use Spotlight to specify criteria to narrow the search results.

- *Use tags:* If you tagged your document, click the Finder icon in the Dock to open a Finder window, then click the tag in the Finder sidebar.
- *Use the Recents folder:* In the sidebar of a Finder window, click Recents.
- *Use the Recent Items menu:* If you worked on a document recently, choose Apple menu > Recent Items.

In some apps, you can open recent documents by choosing File > Open Recent, then the document.

Dictate your messages and documents on Mac

With keyboard dictation, you can dictate text anywhere you can type it. Turn it on in the Dictation pane of Keyboard preferences to enable keyboard dictation—where your words are sent to Apple servers to be analyzed using the latest language data and converted into text in real-time. A feedback window gauges your speaking volume and provides basic dictation controls.

If you need to dictate text and control your Mac using your voice instead of a keyboard and trackpad, use Voice Control.

Note: When Voice Control is on, you can't use keyboard dictation.

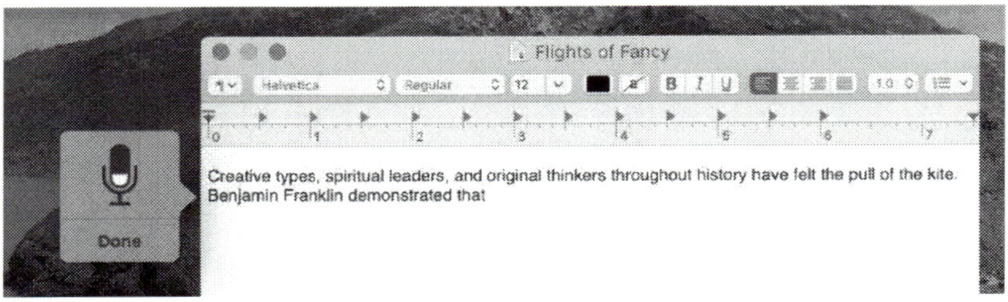

Turn on keyboard dictation

1. On your Mac, choose Apple menu > System Preferences, click Keyboard, then click Dictation.
2. Click On. If a prompt appears, click Enable Dictation.
3. To dictate using another language, click the Language pop-up menu, then choose your language and dialect.
    - *Add an unlisted language:* Choose Customize or Add Language, then select the languages you want to use.
    - *Remove a language:* Click the Language pop-up menu, choose Customize, and then deselect the language you don't want to use.

Dictate text

1. In an app on your Mac, place the insertion point where you want the dictated text to appear.

2. Press the dictation keyboard shortcut or choose Edit > Start Dictation.
3. When the feedback window shows a microphone icon  with a fluctuating loudness indicator, or you hear the tone that signals your Mac is ready for keyboard dictation, dictate your text.

   To insert a punctuation mark, such as a period or comma, say the name of the punctuation mark. You can also perform simple formatting tasks. For example, say "new line" or "new paragraph" to insert space between lines. For a list of the commands you can use while dictating, if you set up keyboard dictation for multiple languages and want to switch languages as you dictate, click the language in the feedback window, then choose the language you want.

   For information about setting up keyboard dictation for multiple languages, see "Turn on keyboard dictation," above.
4. When you're done, press the dictation keyboard shortcut or click done in the feedback window.

Ambiguous text is underlined in blue. If the text is wrong, click it and select an alternate. You can also type or dictate the correct text.

Set a different keyboard dictation shortcut

By default, you press the FN (Function) key twice to start or stop keyboard dictation. If you like, you can choose a different dictation keyboard shortcut.

1. On your Mac, choose Apple menu > System Preferences, click Keyboard, then click Dictation.
2. Click the Shortcut pop-up menu, then choose a different shortcut.

   To create a shortcut that's not in the list, choose Customize, then press the keys you want to use. For example, you could press Option-Z.

Change the microphone used for keyboard dictation

The pop-up menu below the microphone icon in the Dictation pane of Keyboard preferences shows which device your Mac is currently using to listen.

1. On your Mac, choose Apple menu > System Preferences, click Keyboard, then click Dictation.

2. Click the pop-up menu below the microphone icon, then choose the microphone you want to use for keyboard dictation.

   If you choose Automatic, your Mac listens to the device you're most likely to use for keyboard dictation.

Turn off keyboard dictation

- On your Mac, choose Apple menu > System Preferences, click Keyboard, click Dictation, and then click Off.

Take screenshots or screen recordings on Mac

You can take pictures (called *screenshots*) or recordings of the screen on your Mac using Screenshot or keyboard shortcuts. Screenshot provides a panel of tools that let you easily take screenshots and screen recordings, with options to control what you capture—for example, you can set a timer delay or include the pointer or clicks.

Take pictures or screen recordings using Screenshot

1. On your Mac, press Shift-Command-5 (or use Launchpad) to open Screenshot and display the tools.

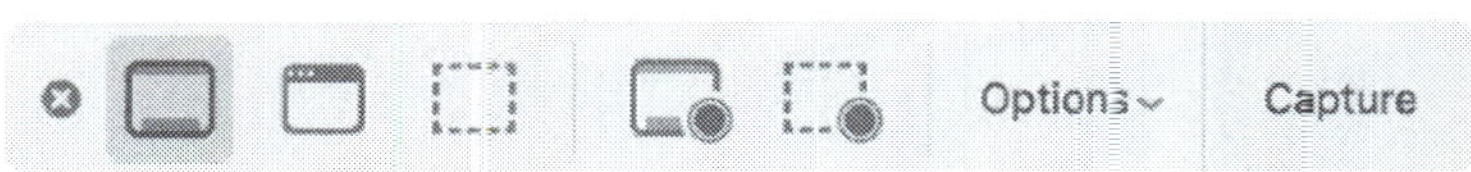

2. Click a tool to use to select what you want to capture or record (or use the Touch Bar).

   For a portion of the screen, drag the frame to reposition it or drag its edges to adjust the size of the area you want to capture or record.

3. Click Options if you want.

   The available options vary based on whether you're taking a screenshot or a screen recording. For example, you can choose to set a timed delay or show the mouse pointer or clicks, and specify where to save the file.

   The Show Floating Thumbnail option helps you work more easily with a completed shot or recording—it floats in the bottom-right corner of the screen for a few seconds so you have time to drag it into a document, mark it up, or share it before it's saved to the location you specified.

4. Start the screenshot or screen recording:

   - *For the entire screen or a portion of it:* Click Capture.
   - *For a window:* Move the cursor to the window, then click the window.

- *For recordings:* Click Record. To stop recording, click the Stop Recording button  in the menu bar.

When the Show Floating Thumbnail option is set, you can do any of the following while the thumbnail is briefly displayed in the bottom-right corner of the screen:

- Swipe right to immediately save the file and make it disappear.
- Drag the thumbnail into a document, an email, a note, or a Finder window.
- Click the thumbnail to open a window where you can mark up the screenshot or trim the recording, or share it.

Depending on where you chose to save the screenshot or recording, an app may open.

Take pictures using keyboard shortcuts

You can use various keyboard shortcuts on your Mac to take pictures of the screen. The files are saved to the desktop.

Tip: To copy a screenshot so you can paste it somewhere—like in an email or to another device—press and hold the Control key while you press the other keys. For example, to copy the whole screen, press Shift-Command-Control-3.

Action	Shortcut
Capture the entire screen	Press Shift-Command-3.
Capture a portion of the screen	Press Shift-Command-4, then move the crosshair pointer to where you want to start the screenshot. Press the mouse or trackpad button, drag over the area you want to capture, then release the mouse or trackpad button.
Capture a window or the menu bar	Press Shift-Command-4, then press the Space bar. Move the camera pointer over the window or the menu bar to highlight it, then click.
Capture a menu and menu items	Open the menu, press Shift-Command-4, and then drag the pointer over the menu items you want to capture.
Open Screenshot	Press Shift-Command 5.

Action	Shortcut
Capture the Touch Bar	Press Shift-Command-6.

You can customize these keyboard shortcuts in the Shortcuts pane of Keyboard preferences. On your Mac, choose Apple menu > System Preferences, click Keyboard, then click Shortcuts.

Screenshots are saved as .png files and screen recordings are saved as .move files. Filenames begin with "Screen Shot" or "Screen Recording" and include the date and time.

You may not be able to take pictures of windows in some apps, such as DVD Player.

View and edit files with Quick Look on Mac

Quick Look offers a fast, full-size preview of nearly any kind of file without opening the file. Just press the Space bar to rotate photos, trim audio and video clips, and use Markup to crop photos and annotate images or PDFs. You can use Quick Look for items in Finder windows, on your desktop, in emails and messages, and other places.

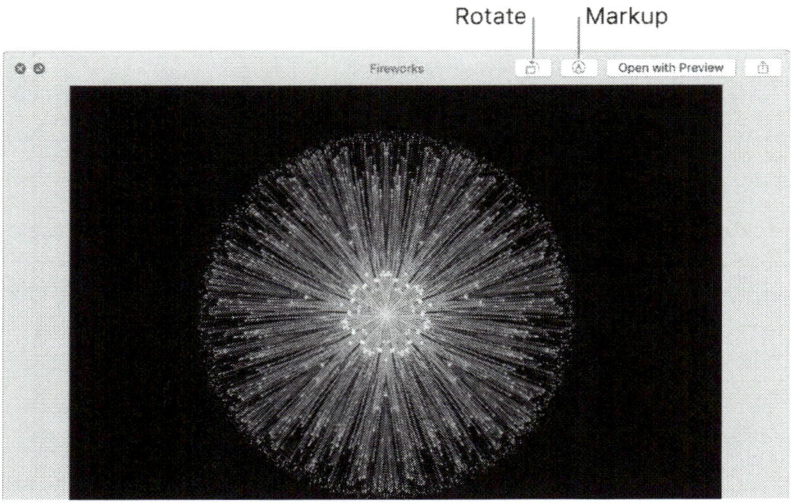

1. On your Mac in a Finder window or on the desktop, select one or more items, then press the Space bar.

   A Quick Look window opens. If you selected multiple items, the first item is shown.

2. In the Quick Look window, do any of the following:

   - *Resize the window:* Drag the corners of the window.

     You can also use Quick Look full screen. Click the Full Screen button in the Quick Look window. To stop using it full screen, move the pointer to the bottom of the window, then click the Exit Full Screen button that appears.

- *Browse items (if you selected multiple items):* Click the arrows near the top-left of the window or press the Left Arrow and Right Arrow keys. In full screen, click the Play button to view the items as a slideshow.
- *Show items in a grid (if you selected multiple items):* Click the Index Sheet button or press Command-Return.
- *Zoom in and out of an item:* Press Command-Plus (+) to make the image bigger or Command-Minus (–) to make it smaller.
- *Rotate an item:* Click the Rotate Left button or press and hold the Option key, then click the Rotate Right button. Keep clicking to continue rotating the item.
- *Mark up an item:* Click the Markup button .
- *Trim an audio or video item:* Click the Trim button, then drag the yellow handles in the trimming bar. To test your changes, click Play. You can start over by clicking Revert.

When you're ready to save your changes, click done, then choose to replace the original file or create a new one.

- *Open an item:* Click Open with [*App*].
- *Share an item:* Click the Share button.

3. When you're done, press the Space bar or click the Close button to close the Quick Look window.

When you open a Live Photo in the Quick Look window, the video portion of the photo plays automatically. To view it again, click Live Photo in the bottom-left corner of the photo.

Mark up files on Mac

Markup on your Mac lets you write, sign, and draw on, or crop or rotate, PDF documents and images. If your iPhone or iPad is nearby, you can use Continuity Markup to mark up the file on your device—even using Apple Pencil on iPad—and instantly see the changes on your Mac.

To use Continuity features, your devices must meet system requirements. See the Apple Support article System requirements for Continuity on Mac, iPhone, iPad, iPod touch, and Apple Watch.

1. When using Quick Look on your Mac, click the Markup tool. Or when using Quick Actions, choose Markup.

   Markup is also available in various apps, such as Mail, Notes, Text Edit, and Photos.

2. Use the tools to mark up an image or a PDF document on your Mac; the tools that are available vary depending on the type of file.

   If your iPhone or iPad is nearby, click the Annotate tool to use Continuity Markup to mark up the file on your device. For information about using

Apple Pencil on iPad, to switch between your markup and the iPad Home screen, swipe up from the bottom of your iPad with one finger. To return to your markup, swipe up from the bottom with one finger to show the iPad Dock, then tap the Sidecar icon .

Note: To duplicate any shape, text, or signature, press and hold the Option key while you drag an item; use the yellow guides to align the items. If you don't like your changes and want to start over, click Revert.

Tool	**Description**
Sketch	Sketch a hape using a single stroke. If your drawing is recognized as a standard shape, it's replaced by that shape; to use your drawing instead, choose it from the palette that's shown.
Draw	Draw a shape using a single stroke. Press your finger more firmly on the trackpad to draw with a heavier, darker line. This tool appears only on computers with a Force Touch trackpad.
Shapes	Click a shape, then drag it where you

Tool	Description
	want. To resize the shape, use the blue handles. If it has green handles, use them to alter the shape. You can zoom and highlight shapes using these tools: • *Loupe*: Drag the loupe to the area you want to magnify. To increase or decrease the magnification, drag the green handle; drag the blue handle to change the loupe size. To further magnify an area, you can create additional loupes and stack them, using the yellow guides to align them. • *Highlight*: Drag the highlight where you want. To resize it, use the blue handles.
Text	Type your text, then drag the text box where you want.
Highlight	Highlight selected text.

Tool	Description
Selection 	
Sign 	If signatures are listed, click one, then drag it where you want. To resize it, use the blue handles. To create a new signature, click the Sign tool, click Create Signature if shown, then click how you want to create your signature: • *Use a trackpad:* Click Trackpad, click the text when asked, sign your name on the trackpad using your finger, and then click done. If you don't like the results, click Clear, then try again. If your trackpad supports it, press your finger more firmly on the trackpad to sign with a heavier, darker line. • *Use your Mac computer's built-in camera:* Click Camera, hold

Tool	Description
	your signature (on white paper) facing the camera so that your signature is level with the blue line in the window. When your signature appears in the window, click done. If you don't like the results, click Clear, then try again. • *Use your iPhone or iPad:* Click Select Device, then choose a device (if more than one is available). On your device, use your finger or Apple Pencil (on iPad) to sign your name, then click done. If you don't like the results, click Clear, then try again.
Shape Style 	Change the thickness and type of lines used in a shape, and add a shadow.
Border Color 	Change the color of the lines used in a shape.

Tool	Description
Fill Color	Change the color that's used inside a shape.
Text Style *A*	Change the font or the font style and color.
Rotate Left or Rotate Right	Click to rotate the item to the left. Continue clicking to keep rotating. To rotate the item to the right, press and hold the Option key, then click until you're done rotating the item.
Crop	Hide part of an item. Drag the corner handles until just the area you want to keep is shown within the frame's border. You can also drag the frame to reposition it. When you're ready, click Crop.
Annotate	Annotate the item using Continuity Markup to sketch or draw on it using your nearby iPhone or iPad. The Annotate tool appears blue

Tool	Description
	when your device is connected; to disconnect your device, click the tool again.

3. When you're finished with your markup, click done.

   If you're working in the Quick Look or Quick Actions window, your changes can't be undone after you close the window.

Combine files into a PDF on Mac

You can quickly combine multiple files into a PDF right from your desktop or a Finder window.

1. On you Mac, click the Finder icon  in the Dock to open a Finder window.
2. Select the files you want to combine into a PDF.

   Alternatively, you can select the files on your desktop.

   Note: The files appear in the PDF in the same order that you select them.
3. Control-click the selected files, then choose Quick Actions > Create PDF.

   The file is created automatically with a name similar to the first file you selected.

Tip: You can also select the files in the Finder and use the Create PDF button in the Preview pane of a Finder window. If you don't see the Preview pane on the right, choose View > Show Preview.

Print documents from your Mac

1. With a document open on your Mac, choose File > Print, or press Command-P.

   The Print dialog opens, with a small preview of how your document will look when printed. Click the arrows below the preview to scroll through the pages.

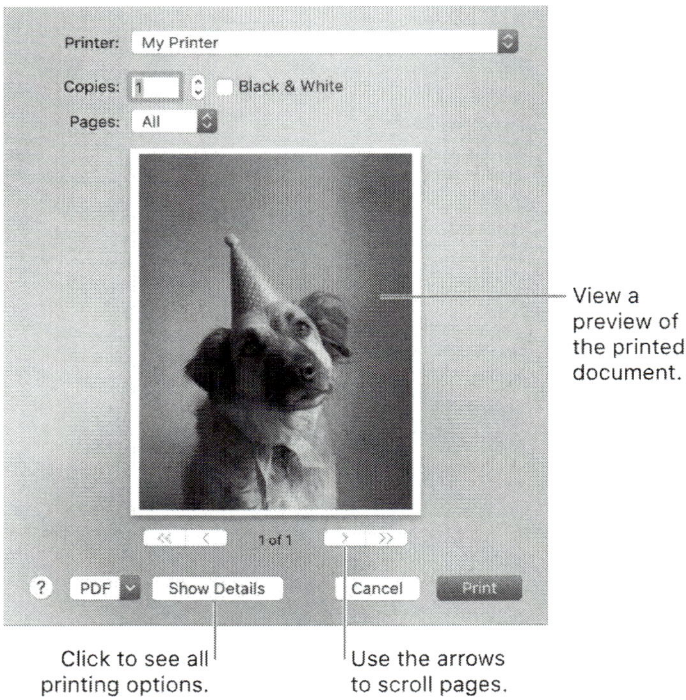

Tip: To view a full-size preview in the Preview app, click the PDF pop-up menu, then choose Open PDF in Preview.

2. If the settings in the Print dialog are fine as is, click Print, and you're done. Otherwise, continue to step 3.
3. Choose any of the following common print settings (you may need to click Show Details to see some of the settings):
    - *Printer:* Choose the printer you want to use. If the printer you want isn't available, you can add one. If you see an icon next to the printer you want to use, there may be an issue you need to resolve—.
    - *Presets:* A preset is a group of print settings. In most cases you can use the default settings, but you can also choose a group of settings you've saved from a previous print job.
    - *Copies:* Specify the number of copies you want. To print all pages of a document before the next copy prints, click Show Details, click the print options pop-up menu, choose Paper Handling, then select "Collate pages."

- *B & W (or Black and White):* Select to print in black and white, if your printer has this capability.
- *Two-Sided:* Select this to print on both sides of the paper (also called *duplexing*), if your printer has this capability.
- *Pages:* Choose to print all pages, a single page, or a range of pages.
- *Orientation:* Click the buttons to switch between portrait or landscape orientation.

For more detailed information about printing options, you might see different options in the Print dialog depending on your printer and the app you're using. If these instructions differ from what you're seeing, check the documentation for the app you're using by clicking Help in the menu bar.

If you print a document and see unexpected margin sizes or clipped text, there may be a conflict between the margins set for your page size in the app and the nonprintable area of the page set for your selected printer. Try setting the nonprintable area for the page size to zero.

Organize files in stacks on Mac

You can use stacks on the desktop to keep files neatly organized in groups. Whenever you save a file to the desktop, it's automatically added to the appropriate stack, helping to keep your desktop clean. The Dockincludes a Downloads stack to group files you download from the internet.

Use stacks on the desktop

You can group stacks by kind (such as images or PDFs), date (such as Date Created or Date Last Opened), or Finder tags. For example, all the documents on your desktop can be grouped in one stack while screenshots are grouped in another.

On your Mac, do any of the following:

- *Turn on stacks:* Click the desktop, then choose View > Use Stacks or press Control-Command-0. You can also Control-click the desktop, then choose Use Stacks.
- *Browse files in a stack:* Swipe left or right on the stack using two fingers on the trackpad; use one finger on a Magic Mouse. You can open the top file in a stack by double-clicking it.
- *Open or close a stack:* Click the stack. You can double-click a file to open it.

- *Change how stacks are grouped:* Click the desktop, choose View > Group Stacks By, then choose an option, such as Date Added. Or Control-click the desktop, choose Group Stacks By, then choose an option.
- *Change how stacks look:* Click the desktop, choose View > Show View Options, then change options. Or Control-click the desktop, then choose Show View Options. You can make icons bigger, change the spacing between icons, move icon labels to the side, or show more information (such as how many files are in a stack).

Use stacks in the Dock

The Dock comes with a Downloads stack where you can easily access items you download from the internet, receive as attachments, or accept using AirDrop.

You can add files and folders to the Dock for quick access, and even display them as a stack. Your Mac creates an alias to the file or folder.

On your Mac, do any of the following:

- *Add files and folders:* Drag and drop a folder to the right of the separator line (after recently used apps, if shown).

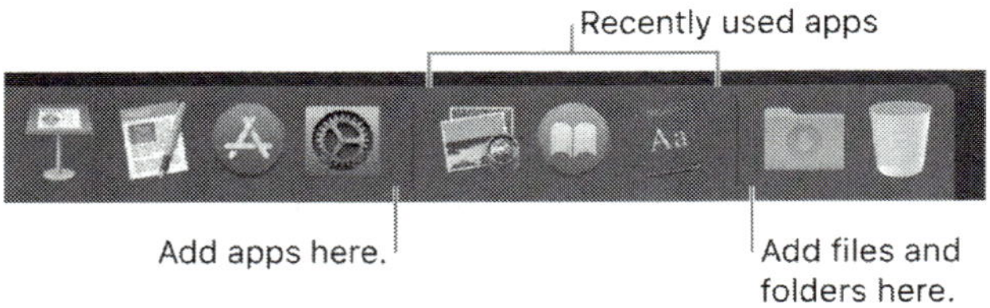

- *Open or close a file or folder:* Click it. When a folder is open, double-click any item to open it. To see a folder in the Finder, click Open in Finder.
- *Change how folders look:* Control-click the folder, then choose how the items in it are sorted, whether to show it in the Dock as a folder or a stack, and how to view its content (such as in a grid or fan).

Organize files in folders on Mac

Everything on your Mac—documents, pictures, music, apps, and more—is organized in folders. As you create documents, install apps, and do other work, you can create new folders to keep yourself organized.

Create a folder

1. On your Mac, click the Finder icon in the Dockto open a Finder window, then navigate to where you want to create the folder.

   Alternatively, click the desktop if you want to create the folder on the desktop.

2. Choose File > New Folder, or press Shift-Command-N.

   If the New Folder command is dimmed, you can't create a folder in the current location.

3. Enter a name for the folder, then press Return.

Move items into folders

1. On your Mac, click the Finder icon in the Dock to open a Finder window.
2. Do any of the following:
   - *Put an item in a folder*: Drag it to the folder.
   - *Put several items in a folder:* Select the items, then drag one of the items to the folder.

     All selected items move to the folder.
   - *Keep an item in its original location and put a copy in a folder:* Select the item, press and hold the Option key, then drag the item to the folder.

- *Keep an item in its original location and put an alias for it in a new folder:* Press and hold the Option and Command keys, then drag the item to the folder to create the alias.
- *Make a copy of an item within the same folder:* Select the item, then choose File > Duplicate or press Command-D.
- *Copy files to a different disk:* Drag the files to the disk.
- *Move files to a different disk:* Press and hold the Command key, then drag the files to the disk.

Quickly group multiple items into a new folder

You can quickly create a folder of items on the desktop or in a Finder window.

1. On your Mac, select all the items you want to group together.
2. Control-click one of the selected items, then choose New Folder with Selection.
3. Enter a name for the folder, then press Return.

Merge two folders with the same name

If you have two folders with identical names at two different locations, you can merge them into a single folder.

- On your Mac, press and hold the Option key, then drag one folderto the location that contains a folder with the same name. In the dialog that appears, click Merge.

  The Merge option appears only if one of the folders contains items that are not in the other folder. If the folders contain different versions of identically named files, the only options are Stop or Replace.

To organize your files automatically, use Smart Folders. Smart Folders automatically gather files by type and subject matter, and are instantly updated as you change, add, and remove files on your Mac.

Use tags to organize files on Mac

You can tag files and folders to make them easier to find. Tags work with all your files and folders, whether you store them on your Mac or keep them in iCloud.

Ask Siri. Say something like: “Find files that are tagged red.”

Tag files and folders

You can add multiple tags to any file or folder.

On your Mac, do any of the following:

- *Tag an open file:* Hold the pointer to the right of the document title, click the arrow, click in the Tags field, then enter a new tag, or choose one from the list.
- *Tag a new file when you save it:* Click File > Save. In the Save dialog, click in the Tags field, then enter a new tag, or choose one from the list.
- *Tag a file on the desktop or in the Finder:* Select the item, then open the File menu. You can also Control-click the item, or tap it with two fingers. Choose a color below Tags, or click Tags to choose from more tags or enter a new tag.

  In a Finder window, you can also select the item, click the Tags button , then enter a new tag, or choose one from the list.

Tip: Use keyboard shortcuts to tag files quickly—select a file, then use Control-1 through Control-7 to add (or remove) your favorite tags. Control-0 (zero) removes all tags from a file.

Find items you tagged

1. On your Mac, click the Finder icon in the Dockto open a Finder window.
2. Do any of the following:

- *Search for a tag:* Enter the tag color or name in the search field, then select the tag from the suggestions.
- *Select a tag in the sidebar:* To see everything with a certain tag, click the tag in the Finder sidebar.

  To change the items you see in the sidebar, choose Finder > Preferences, click Tags, then select the tags you want to see.
- *Group items by a tag:* Click the Group button , then choose Tags.
- *Sort items by a tag:* In any view, choose View > Show View Options, click the Sort by pop-up menu, then choose Tags. In List view, select the Tags checkbox to display the column, move the pointer over the Tags column, and then click it. Click the column name again to reverse the sort order.

Remove tags

On your Mac, do one of the following:

- *Remove tags from an item:* Control-click the item or tap it with two fingers, then click Tags. Select the tags you want to remove, then press Delete.
- *Remove tags from your Mac:* In the Finder, choose Finder > Preferences, then click Tags. Select the tags you want to remove, then click the Remove button.

Edit tags

1. In the Finder  on your Mac, choose Finder > Preferences, then click Tags.
2. Do any of the following:
    - *See a tag in the Finder sidebar:* Select the blue checkbox to the right of the tag.
    - *Change a tag color:* Click the color next to the tag, then choose a new color.
    - *Change a tag name:* Click the tag, click the tag's name, and then enter a new name.
    - *Create a new tag:* Click the Add button.
    - *Delete a tag:* Select the tag, then click the Remove button.

- *Add a tag to the shortcut menu:* Select the tag in the list, then drag it over the tag you want to replace in the favorites section at the bottom of the window. There can be up to seven tags in the shortcut menu that appears when you Control-click a file.
- *Remove a tag from the shortcut menu:* Drag the tag out of the Favorite Tags section until you see the remove sign  .

Back up your files with Time Machine on Mac

With Time Machine, you can back up your entire Mac, including system files, apps, music, photos, emails, and documents. When Time Machine is turned on, it automatically backs up your Mac and performs hourly, daily, and weekly backups of your files.

When you use Time Machine on a computer using Apple File System (APFS), Time Machine not only keeps a copy of everything on your backup disk, it also saves *local snapshots* of files that have changed on your internal disk, so you can recover previous versions. These local snapshots are saved hourly (unless you deselect Back up automatically) and they're stored on your computer's internal disk.

Note: If you're using APFS, local snapshots are created on your APFS disk, regardless of whether the disk is on a portable or desktop Mac.

If you accidentally delete or change a file, you can use Time Machine to recover it.

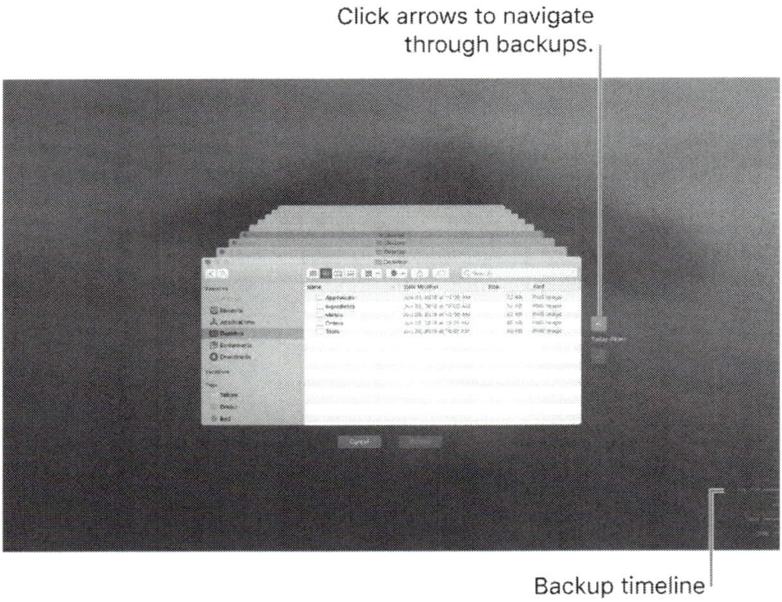

Even though Time Machine creates local snapshots on computers using APFS, you should also back up your files to a location other than your internal disk, such as an external hard disk, a disk on your network, or a Time Capsule. That way, if anything ever happens to your internal disk or to your Mac, you can restore your entire system to another Mac.

1. Connect an external hard disk to your Mac and turn the disk on.

   You're asked if you want to use the disk to back up your Mac.

2. On your Mac, click Use as Backup Disk, then follow the instructions in Time Machine preferences.

   To open Time Machine preferences, choose Apple menu > System Preferences, then click Time Machine.

Note: If you create a backup on a Mac or partition with macOS Catalina, you can only use that backup on Mac computers or partitions with macOS Catalina.

Restore items backed up with Time Machine on Mac

If you use Time Machine to back up the files on your Mac, you can easily get back lost items or recover older versions of files. You can use Time Machine within many apps.

1. On your Mac, open a window for the item you want to restore.

   For example, to recover a file you accidentally deleted from your Documents folder, open the Documents folder. To recover an email message, open your inbox in Mail.

If you're missing an item from the desktop, you don't need to open a window.

2. Use Launchpad to view and open apps on Mac and open Time Machine. A message may appear while your Mac connects to the backup disk.

   You can also open Time Machine by clicking the Time Machine icon in the menu bar, then choosing Enter Time Machine. If the Time Machine icon isn't in the menu bar, choose Apple menu > System Preferences, click Time Machine, then select "Show Time Machine in menu bar."

3. Use the arrows and timeline to browse the local snapshots and backups.

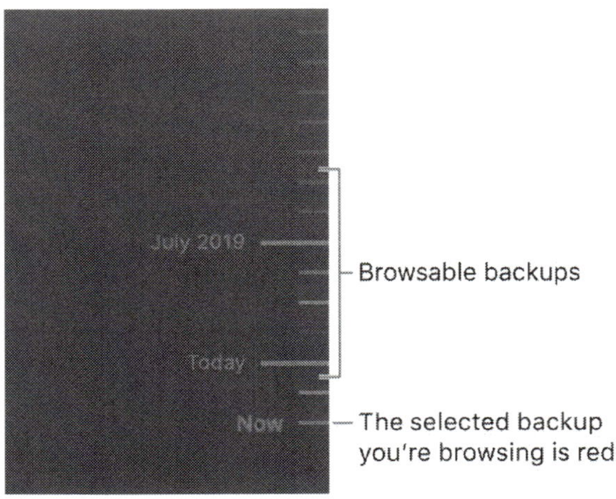

If you see a pulsing light to semi-dark gray tick mark, it represents a backup that's still loading or validating on the backup disk.

4. Select one or more items you want to restore (these can include folders or your entire disk), then click Restore.

   Restored items return to their original location. For example, if an item was in the Documents folder, it's returned to the Documents folder.

With many apps, you can use Time Machine within individual documents, so you can examine and read past versions to find the version you want. You can use iCloud Drive and iCloud Photos to safely store your documents, photos, and videos in iCloud.

Chapter 5

Apple ID and iCloud

Create an Apple ID on Mac

An Apple ID gives you access to the iTunes Store, the App Store, Apple Books, iCloud, FaceTime, and other Apple services. It consists of an email address (for example, michael_cavanna@icloud.com) and a password. Apple recommends you use the same Apple ID for all Apple services. For more information about Apple ID You can create an Apple ID using your current email address or have an @iCloud email address generated for you.

You can create an Apple ID on a Mac, an iOS or iPadOS device, or at the Apple ID account website. See the Apple Support article Sign in with your Apple ID.

Using either your current email address or an iCloud address generated for you, create an Apple ID:

1. On your Mac, choose Apple menu > System Preferences, then click Sign In.
2. Click Create Apple ID, then follow the onscreen instructions.

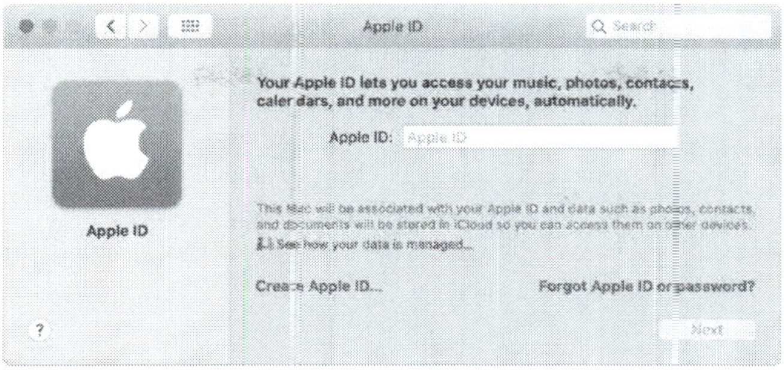

Note: In several countries and regions, you can use a phone number instead of an email address as your Apple ID. See the Apple Support article Use your mobile phone number as your Apple ID.

For information about setting up your Apple ID preferences on your Mac,

To keep your purchases and access to Apple services secure, don't share your Apple ID and password with others. To share your purchases with family members, you can set up a Family Sharing group with up to six members of your family.

For information about using your Apple ID on an iOS or iPadOS device, see "Manage Apple ID and iCloud settings" in the user guide for iPhone, iPad, or iPod touch.

Use two-factor authentication for security on your Mac, iOS devices, and iPadOS devices

Two-factor authentication is an extra layer of security for your Apple ID designed to ensure that you're the only one who can access your account—even if someone knows your password.

Turn on two-factor authentication for your Apple ID

Apple IDs created with macOS 10.12.4 or later, iOS 10.3 or later, or iPadOS are protected with two-factor authentication automatically. When you sign in to your account, you see that two-factor authentication is already on. If it is not on, you can turn on two-factor authentication while setting up a new Mac, or follow the steps below any time to turn it on in Password & Security preferences.

1. On your Mac, choose Apple menu > System Preferences, click Apple ID, then select Password & Security in the sidebar.
2. Click Set up Two-Factor Authentication, then click Continue.
3. Answer the verification questions, then click Verify.
4. Enter your phone number for verification, select a verification method, and then click Continue.
5. When asked, verify your identity with the six-digit verification code sent to your trusted phone. You won't be asked for a verification code again on your Mac unless you sign out your Apple ID completely,

erase your Mac, or need to change your password for security reasons.

Sign in to a new device or browser with two-factor authentication

A verification code is a temporary code sent to your trusted devices or phone number when you sign in to a new device or browser with your Apple ID.

1. When you're asked for the verification code, look for a notification at a trusted phone number or on any of your trusted devices.

   To send the code to a trusted phone number, click "Didn't get a verification code?" in the notification, then choose the phone number.

2. On a trusted device, tap or click Allow to see the code on that device.
3. Enter the code on your Mac.

Get a verification code on a Mac, even when it's offline

If you can't receive a verification code on your phone or trusted devices, or if none of them are available, you can get a verification code in Password & Security preferences, even if your Mac is offline.

1. On your Mac, choose Apple menu > System Preferences, click Apple ID, then select Password & Security in the sidebar.
2. Click Get Verification Code.
3. Write down the verification code or enter it in the notification, then click OK.

Add a trusted device

To make a Mac (macOS 10.11 or later), an iOS device (iOS 9), or an iPadOS device a trusted device, you must sign in using your Apple ID on the Mac or device.

- *Adding a Mac (macOS Catalina):* Choose Apple menu > System Preferences, then click Sign In and enter your Apple ID. Follow the onscreen instructions.
- *Adding a Mac (macOS Mojave or earlier):* Choose Apple menu > System Preferences, click iCloud, then click Sign In and enter your Apple ID. Follow the onscreen instructions.
- *Adding an iOS or iPadOS device:* Tap Settings >*your name* at the top of the screen. (If you're using a device with iOS 10.2 or earlier, tap Settings >

iCloud.) Verify your identity with a six-digit verification code.

If you previously signed in to your Mac, iOS, or iPadOS device using a different Apple ID, sign out, then sign in again.

You won't be asked for a verification code again on that device unless you sign out of your Apple ID completely, erase your device, or need to change your password for security reasons.

Add or remove a trusted phone number

You must verify at least one trusted phone number to enroll in two-factor authentication.

1. On your Mac, choose Apple menu > System Preferences, click Apple ID, then select Password & Security in the sidebar.
2. Do any of the following:
   - To add a phone number, click the Add button +. Enter your Mac login password. Enter a phone number that can be used to verify your identity. Select whether you want to be reached by text or phone call, then click Continue. Enter the code sent to the email address or

phone number and click next. Your trusted phone numbers appear in a list.

- To remove an email or phone number, select a phone number, click the Delete button —, and then click Remove.

View or remove trusted devices

1. On your Mac, choose Apple menu > System Preferences, then click Apple ID.

   A list of your trusted devices appears at the bottom of the sidebar.

2. Do any of the following:
   - *View details of a trusted device:* Select a device in the list to see details about it.
   - *Remove a trusted device:* Select a device in the list, click Remove from Account, then click Remove.

If you already use two-factor authentication, you can no longer turn it off. Certain features in the latest versions of iOS, iPadOS, and macOS require this extra level of security. If you recently updated your account to turn on two-factor authentication and then decide not to use it, you must stop using it within 2 weeks. Open your enrollment confirmation email and click the link to return to your previous security settings.

You can manage your trusted devices and phone numbers by signing in to your Apple ID account page.

Set up your Apple ID preferences

Use your Apple ID to sign in to your Apple ID preferences. Your Apple ID gives you access to all Apple services, including iTunes Store, Book Store, App Store, iCloud, and other Apple services. After you sign in, you can use Apple ID preferences to change your account name, photo, contact information, password and security settings, payment and shipping information, and more.

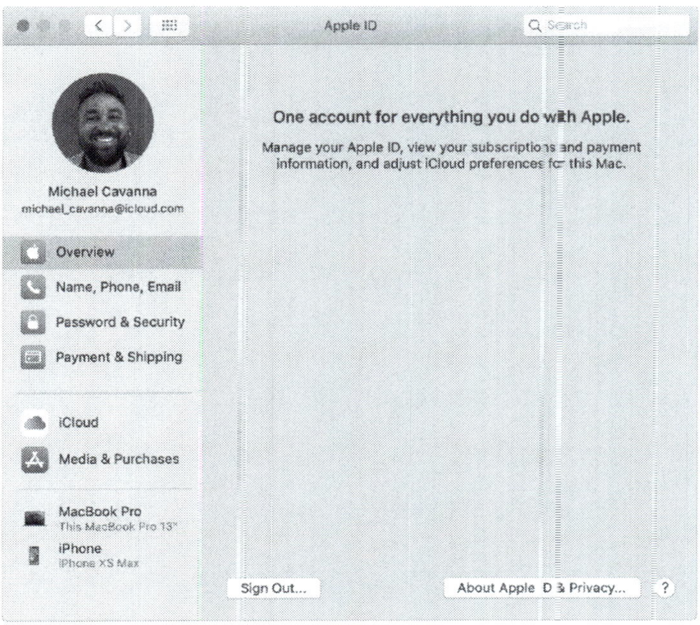

Use the following sidebar items to set up your Apple ID preferences on your Mac:

- *Overview:* Use these options to review Apple ID & Privacy policy and sign out of your Apple ID. *Name, Phone, Email:* Use these options to enter your name, phone number, email information, and other contact information associated with your Apple ID.
- *Password & Security:* Use these options to change the password and security settings associated with your Apple ID.
- *Payment & Shipping:* Use these options to set up the payment and shipping information associated with your Apple ID.
- *ICloud:* Use these options to select the iCloud features you want and manage iCloud storage.
- *Media & Purchases:* Use these options to change the media and purchases settings associated with your Apple ID.
- *Trusted devices:* Use this list to review the trusted devices that use your Apple ID and select and change a trusted device's options.

Set up iCloud features on Mac

At any time after you sign in to your Apple ID, you can select the iCloud features you want to use.

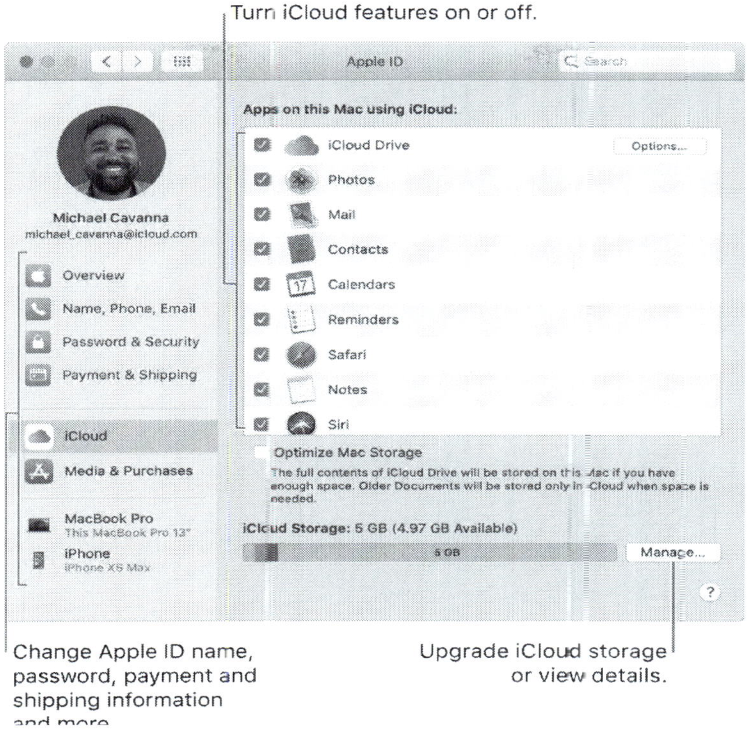

Important: To set up Messages in iCloud to share all your messages across devices, open Messages on your Mac, choose Messages > Preferences, click I Message, then select the Enable Messages in iCloud checkbox. To set up iCloud features on your iOS or iPadOS device, Apple TV, or Windows computer, see the Apple Support article Change your iCloud feature settings.

Turn iCloud features on or off

1. On your Mac, choose Apple menu > System Preferences, click Apple ID, then select iCloud in the sidebar.

2. Select the app whose iCloud features you want to use. Deselect any app whose iCloud features you don't want to use.

   Some features have additional settings you can change by clicking Options or Details near the feature name when the feature is turned on.

   If you select the Contacts feature while your Contacts app is synced with Google Contacts, Google syncing is turned off. You should keep it turned off while using iCloud for your contacts.

Turn on iCloud Photos

1. On your Mac, choose Apple menu > System Preferences, click Apple ID, then select iCloud in the sidebar.
2. Select Photos.

For more information about setting up iCloud in Photos,

Change iCloud Keychain options

If your Apple ID is set up for two-factor authentication you are done setting up iCloud Keychain when you select it in the iCloud apps list. When you set up iCloud on a new device, you can allow the device to use your iCloud data simply by entering the login password or passcode on a device that already has iCloud set up.

Follow the instructions below if a Options button appears beside the iCloud Keychain option.

1. On your Mac, choose Apple menu > System Preferences, click Apple ID, then select iCloud in the sidebar.
2. Click the Options button next to Keychain, and select any of the following:
    - Whether your iCloud Security Code can be used to approve iCloud Keychain on new devices.
    - The iCloud Security Code and the phone number used to verify your identity after you use the iCloud Security Code.
3. If “Waiting for approval” appears below Keychain, click Options to enter your iCloud Security Code instead of approving this Mac from another device.

Change Find My Mac details

1. On your Mac, choose Apple menu > System Preferences, click Apple ID, then select iCloud in the sidebar.

2. If “Location Services is off” appears below Find My Mac, click Details, then follow the onscreen instructions so you can locate this Mac.

To set up iCloud on your iOS or iPadOS device, or Windows computer, see the Apple Support article Set up iCloud on your iPhone, iPad, or iPod touch.

Use iCloud Drive to store documents on your Mac, iPhone, and iPad

With iCloud Drive, you can safely store all kinds of documents in iCloud, and access them from all your computers, and iOS and iPadOS devices. If you like, you can have all the files in your desktop and documents folders stored automatically in iCloud Drive. That way, you can save files right where you usually keep them, and they become available on all your computers, and iOS and iPadOS devices.

You can use iCloud Drive on Mac computers (OS X 10.10 or later), iOS devices (iOS 8 or later), iPadOS devices, and Windows computers with iCloud for Windows (Windows 7 or later required). You must be signed in to iCloud using the same Apple IDon all your computers and devices.

You can also use iCloud Drive on iCloud.com from a web browser on a Mac or Windows computer.

To set up iCloud drive using an iOS or iPadOS device, Windows PC, or on iCloud.com, see the Apple Support article Set up iCloud Drive.

Set up iCloud Drive

If you haven't yet set up iCloud Drive on this Mac, you can do it now in the iCloud pane of Apple ID preferences.

1. On your Mac, choose Apple menu > System Preferences, click Apple ID, then select iCloud in the sidebar.
2. Select iCloud Drive.

The first time you select the iCloud Drive feature on any of your devices, you're asked to upgrade. When you upgrade, your documents and data currently stored in iCloud are moved to iCloud Drive. If you're not asked to upgrade, your account is already upgraded.

Important: After upgrading to iCloud Drive, your documents stored in iCloud Drive are only available on your computers, and iOS and iPadOS devices that meet minimum system requirements, and have iCloud Drive turned on. Your documents in iCloud Drive are also available on iCloud.com.

If you have devices with iCloud Drive turned off, documents and data on those devices aren't kept up to date with documents and data on your devices with iCloud Drive turned on.

Store your Desktop and Documents folders in iCloud Drive

1. On your Mac, choose Apple menu > System Preferences, click Apple ID, select iCloud in the sidebar, then click Options next to iCloud Drive.

   If you don't see Options next to iCloud Drive, make sure iCloud Drive is turned on.

2. Select Desktop & Documents Folders.
3. Click Done.

After you select Desktop & Documents Folders, you're Desktop and Documents folders are moved into iCloud Drive. They also appear in the iCloud Drive section of the Finder sidebar.

If you can't move or save a document to iCloud Drive

If you can't move or save a document to iCloud Drive, your iCloud storage space may be full. The document stays on your Mac, and is uploaded to iCloud Drive when space becomes available.

ICloud Drive shares your iCloud storage with iCloud Photos, iOS and iPadOS device backups, messages and attachments in iCloud Mail (your @icloud.com email account), and more.

To get more space, do the following:

- Upgrade your storage. Remove items you don't need to store in iCloud Drive.

Use iCloud File Sharing to share documents with other iCloud users

With iCloud File Sharing, you can share any kind of file or document in iCloud Drive with other iCloud users. You and the people you invite can view and even work on your documents. The people who receive your invitation can click a link to download the shared file from iCloud to any of their devices. Everyone views the same shared document. If you allow others to make edits, they can change and save the document and you see the updates the next time you open the document on your Mac.

For information about iCloud Drive and setting it up on your Mac.

Share documents

1. To share a document, do one of the following:

- In the Finder on your Mac, select iCloud Drive, select a document, click the Share button, then choose Add People.

  Tip: If the item is on the desktop, Control-click it, choose Share from the shortcut menu, then choose Add People.

- In an app that supports iCloud File Sharing, open a document, click the Share button, then choose Add People.

2. Select the app you want to use to send the invitation.

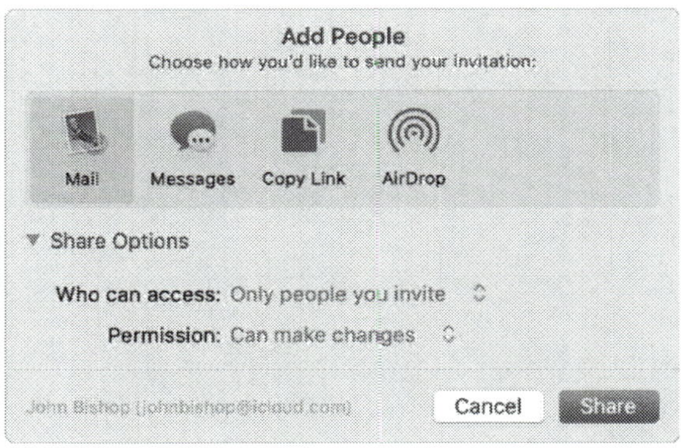

   You can use Mail, Messages, Copy Link, and Airdrop to send an invitation.

3. Click the disclosure triangle next to Share Options, click the "Who can access" pop-up menu, then do one of the following:

- Choose "Only people you invite" to allow only invitees to access the document.
- Choose "Anyone with link" to allow anyone who receives the link to access the document. For example, your invitees can share the link and give access to others not included in the original invitation.

4. Click the Permission pop-up menu, then do one of the following:
   - Choose "Can make changes" to allow others to revise the document.
   - Choose "View only" to allow read-only access.
5. Click Share, then add the email addresses of the people you want to share with.

When the invitees receive your invitation, they can download the shared file from iCloud to any of their devices. If you allow it, they can make changes and save the document. You see the updates the next time you open the file on your Mac.

Accept an invitation and revise a document

When you download a document that you've been invited to share, the shared file is available in iCloud Drive on your Mac, the Files app (iOS 11 or later or iPadOS) or the iCloud

Drive app (on a device with iOS 10 or earlier or iPadOS), on iCloud.com, and on a PC with iCloud for Windows.

If you have permission to revise the document, you can open it with any compatible app, then make and save your changes.

1. In the invitation, click the link to the shared document.

   If necessary, sign in with your Apple ID and password.

2. When the file opens in an app on your Mac, make your changes, then save the document.

   You can also open the file later with any compatible app and make changes. Anyone sharing the document sees the latest changes to the file the next time they open it.

Change the sharing options of a document

You can change the sharing settings you chose after you share a document.

1. On your Mac, select the document in iCloud Drive, or open it in an app that supports iCloud File Sharing, click the Share button 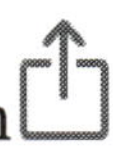, then choose Show People.
2. Do any of the following:

- *Share a document with more people:* Click the Add People button, then add an email address for each new invitee.
- *Copy a link to the shared file to send to another person:* Click the disclosure triangle next to Shared Options, then click Copy Link. You can now paste the link into an email or other app.
- *Change who can access the file to download:* Click the disclosure triangle next to Share Options, then choose “Only people you invite” to only allow invitees to access the document, or choose “Anyone with link” to allow anyone who receives the link to access the document.
- *Change whether the shared document can be changed or viewed only:* Click the disclosure triangle next to Share Options, then choose “Can make changes” to allow others to revise the document, or choose “View only” to allow read-only access.
- *Change the sharing settings for a specific person:* Position the pointer over a person’s name, click , then choose the settings you want.

- *Stop sharing a file with a specific person:* Position the pointer over the person's name, click, then choose Remove Access.

Stop sharing a document

You can stop sharing files with people you invited.

1. On your Mac, select the document in iCloud Drive or open it in an app that supports iCloud File Sharing.
2. Click the Share button, then choose Show People.
3. Do any of the following:
   - *Stop sharing with everyone:* Click the disclosure triangle next to Share Options, then click Stop Sharing.
   - *Stop sharing with a specific person:* Hold the pointer over the person's name, click, then choose Remove Access.

You can also simply move or delete the document from iCloud Drive to stop others from having access to it.

Use iCloud File Sharing to share documents with other iCloud users

With iCloud File Sharing, you can share any kind of file or document in iCloud Drive with other iCloud users. You and the people you invite can view and even work on your documents. The people who receive your invitation can click a link to download the shared file from iCloud to any of their devices. Everyone views the same shared document. If you allow others to make edits, they can change and save the document and you see the updates the next time you open the document on your Mac.

For information about iCloud Drive and setting it up on your Mac.

Share documents

1. To share a document, do one of the following:
    - In the Finder on your Mac, select iCloud Drive, select a document, click the Share button, then choose Add People.

      Tip: If the item is on the desktop, Control-click it, choose Share from the shortcut menu, then choose Add People.
    - In an app that supports iCloud File Sharing, open a document, click the Share button, then choose Add People.
2. Select the app you want to use to send the invitation.

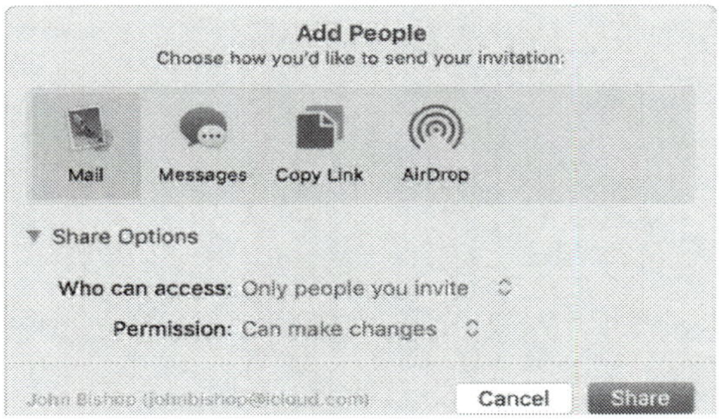

You can use Mail, Messages, Copy Link, and Airdrop to send an invitation.

3. Click the disclosure triangle next to Share Options, click the "Who can access" pop-up menu, then do one of the following:
    - Choose "Only people you invite" to allow only invitees to access the document.
    - Choose "Anyone with link" to allow anyone who receives the link to access the document. For example, your invitees can share the link and give access to others not included in the original invitation.
4. Click the Permission pop-up menu, then do one of the following:
    - Choose "Can make changes" to allow others to revise the document.
    - Choose "View only" to allow read-only access.

5. Click Share, then add the email addresses of the people you want to share with.

When the invitees receive your invitation, they can download the shared file from iCloud to any of their devices. If you allow it, they can make changes and save the document. You see the updates the next time you open the file on your Mac.

Accept an invitation and revise a document

When you download a document that you've been invited to share, the shared file is available in iCloud Drive on your Mac, the Files app (iOS 11 or later or iPadOS) or the iCloud Drive app (on a device with iOS 10 or earlier or iPadOS), on iCloud.com, and on a PC with iCloud for Windows.

If you have permission to revise the document, you can open it with any compatible app, then make and save your changes.

1. In the invitation, click the link to the shared document.

   If necessary, sign in with your Apple ID and password.

2. When the file opens in an app on your Mac, make your changes, then save the document.

You can also open the file later with any compatible app and make changes. Anyone sharing the document sees the latest changes to the file the next time they open it.

Change the sharing options of a document

You can change the sharing settings you chose after you share a document.

1. On your Mac, select the document in iCloud Drive, or open it in an app that supports iCloud File Sharing, click the Share button, then choose Show People.
2. Do any of the following:
    - *Share a document with more people:* Click the Add People button, then add an email address for each new invitee.
    - *Copy a link to the shared file to send to another person:* Click the disclosure triangle next to Shared Options, then click Copy Link. You can now paste the link into an email or other app.
    - *Change who can access the file to download:* Click the disclosure triangle next to Share Options, then choose "Only people you invite" to only allow invitees to access the document,

or choose "Anyone with link" to allow anyone who receives the link to access the document.

- *Change whether the shared document can be changed or viewed only:* Click the disclosure triangle next to Share Options, then choose "Can make changes" to allow others to revise the document, or choose "View only" to allow read-only access.
- *Change the sharing settings for a specific person:* Position the pointer over a person's name, click, then choose the settings you want.
- *Stop sharing a file with a specific person:* Position the pointer over the person's name, click, then choose Remove Access.

Stop sharing a document

You can stop sharing files with people you invited.

1. On your Mac, select the document in iCloud Drive or open it in an app that supports iCloud File Sharing.
2. Click the Share button, then choose Show People.
3. Do any of the following:

- *Stop sharing with everyone:* Click the disclosure triangle next to Share Options, then click Stop Sharing.
- *Stop sharing with a specific person:* Hold the pointer over the person's name, click , then choose Remove Access.

You can also simply move or delete the document from iCloud Drive to stop others from having access to it.

Manage iCloud storage on Mac

When you sign up for iCloud, you automatically get 5 GB of free storage. Your iCloud storage is used for documents stored in iCloud Drive, iCloud Photos, iOS and iPadOS device backups, messages and attachments in iCloud Mail (your @icloud.com email account), and more. If you run out of space, you can upgrade your storage. You can also remove stored items to make more space available.

View and manage iCloud storage

1. On your Mac, choose Apple menu > System Preferences, click Apple ID, then select iCloud in the sidebar.
2. Click Manage, then do any of the following:
   - *Upgrade your storage:* Click Buy More Storage or Change Storage Plan, choose the

amount of storage you want, then follow the instructions.

When you buy an iCloud storage upgrade, it's billed to your Apple ID account. If you're in a Family Sharing group and you use the same Apple ID to share family purchases, the upgrade is billed to the family organizer's account.

- *See how an app or feature is using storage:* Select an app or feature on the left, then read the usage information on the right.
- *Remove an iOS or iPadOS device backup:* Click Backups on the left, select a device on the right whose backup you don't need, then click Delete (below the list of backups). If you don't see Backups on the left, your iOS or iPadOS device doesn't have iCloud backups.

  WARNING: If you delete the iCloud backup for your current iOS or iPadOS device, iCloud stops automatically backing up the device.
- *Turn off Siri and remove Siri-related data:* Select Siri on the left, then click Disable and Delete.

3. Click Done.

Delete items from iCloud storage

You can permanently remove all documents and data for an app, remove documents individually, and also recover files you deleted from iCloud Drive in the last 30 days. You can save copies of documents before removing them from iCloud.

Use iCloud Photos to store photos in iCloud

With iCloud Photos, all the photos and videos in your photo library are stored in iCloud, so you can access them from your Mac, PC, iPhone, iPad, or Apple TV, and on iCloud.com.

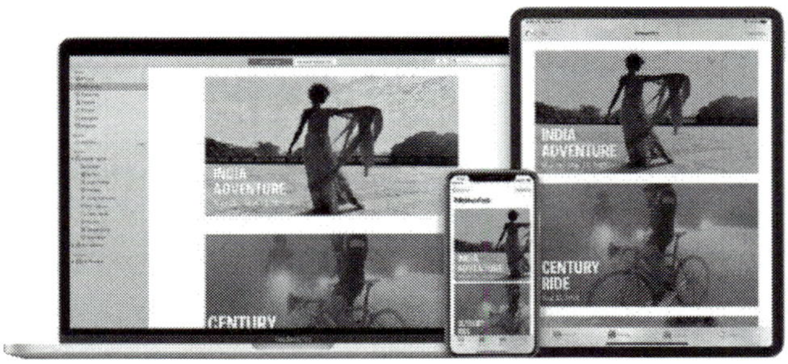

Any new photos and videos you add to Photos, or take with an iPhone or iPad, appear on all your devices that have iCloud Photos turned on. Your photos and albums are organized the same way on every device, and if you make edits or remove items, you see the changes on all your devices.

Before you set up iCloud Photos, update to the latest version of macOS, or the latest version of iOS or iPadOS on your device.

Turn on iCloud Photos

If you're not already signed in with your Apple ID, choose Apple menu > System Preferences, click "Sign in," then enter your Apple ID and password. Click iCloud in the Apple ID preferences sidebar, then select Photos in the list of apps.

1. In the Photos app on your Mac, choose Photos > Preferences, then click iCloud.
2. Select the iCloud Photos checkbox.

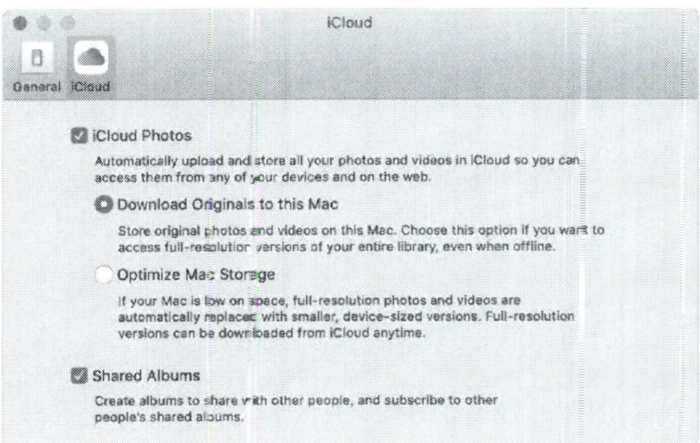

3. Select one of the following options:

- *Download Originals to this Mac:* Stores the full-size versions of your photos both on your Mac and in iCloud.
- *Optimiz Mac Storage:* Stores smaller versions of your photos on your Mac when storage space is limited, and keeps the original, full-size photos in iCloud. Choose this option to conserve space on your Mac. To restore the originals to your Mac, just select "Download Originals to this Mac."

  Note: If this option is selected and you run low on storage space, only the still image of a Live Photo is stored on your Mac. When you open a Live Photo, the video portion is downloaded from iCloud so you can play it.

When you first turn on iCloud Photos, it can take a while to upload your photos to iCloud. You can continue to use Photos while your photos are being uploaded.

Tip: To temporarily pause uploading or downloading of photos and videos with iCloud Photos, click Photos in the sidebar, click Days in the toolbar, then click the Pause button at the bottom of the Days view. Photos pauses uploading and downloading for 24 hours and then resumes automatically.

ICloud Photos doesn't store your projects or Smart Albums in iCloud or on your iPhone or iPad. (Smart Albums are shared with your other Mac computers, however.) To keep a backup of your projects and Smart Albums, make sure you back up the library to another storage device.

You can have multiple photo libraries, but iCloud Photos keeps only the photos and videos in the System Photo Library up to date.

Stop using iCloud Photos

Important: If you turn off iCloud Photos, you'll be prompted to select "Download Originals to this Mac" in the iCloud pane of Photos preferences so that all your original photos can be downloaded to your Mac. Be sure to allow time for your originals to download before turning off iCloud Photos.

1. In the Photos app on your Mac, choose Photos > Preferences, then click iCloud.
2. Deselect the iCloud Photos checkbox.
3. If you want to turn off iCloud Photos on all your devices, open Apple ID preferences in System Preferences, select iCloud in the sidebar, click the Manage button, click Photos, then click "Turn off and Delete."

After you turn off iCloud Photos on your Mac, edits you make to photos on your Mac don't appear on your other devices, and new photos and videos you take aren't added to Photos on your Mac. Your library remains in iCloud and available to other devices that use iCloud Photos.

If you don't use iCloud Photos on your Mac, you can sync your Mac and a connected iPhone or iPad to transfer photos..

WARNING: If you turn off iCloud Photos on all your devices, your photos and videos will be deleted from iCloud in 30 days, and you won't be able to recover them, unless you click Undo Delete before that time.

Chapter 6

Family and Friends

Set up Family Sharing on Mac

Family Sharing lets up to six members of your family share iTunes Store, App Store, and Apple Books purchases, an iCloud storage plan—all without sharing accounts. Your family can share subscriptions to Apple Music, Apple TV, Apple News+, and Apple Arcade (not available in all countries or regions). Your family can also share a photo album, a family calendar, and help locate each other's' devices with the Find My app on theMac, on iCloud.com, and on iOS and iPadOS devices.

One adult—the family organizer—sets up Family Sharing and invites up to five people to join the Family Sharing group. Choose Apple menu > System Preferences, and do one of the following:

- *If you have signed in to your Apple ID:* Click Family Sharing.
- *If you have not signed in to your Apple ID:* Click Sign In. Enter your Apple ID information according to the onscreen instructions. After signing in, click at the top of the System Preferences window, then click Family Sharing, which now appears next to the Apple ID preferences.

2. Select Family in the sidebar.
3. To add yourself as the family organizer and add family members to your Family Sharing group, click the Add button , then do one of the following:
   - *Add someone who has an Apple ID:* Enter the name or email address of the person you want to join the family, click Continue, then follow the onscreen instructions.

     If the person you're adding is nearby, they can simply enter their Apple ID and password.

Otherwise, you can email the person an invitation to join.

- *Create an Apple ID for a child under 13:* Select "Create an Apple ID for a child who doesn't have an account," click Continue, then follow the onscreen instructions.

4. To add another member, repeat step 3.
5. To select the apps and services that you want your family to share, do any of the following:

   - *Set up Purchase Sharing:* Select Purchase Sharing in the sidebar, then select your options. Your family can share purchases from the iTunes Store, the App Store, and Apple Books so everyone has access to them. All purchases are made through the shared payment method you set up. You can change the account used to make purchases and decline to share your purchases with family members.
   - *Upgrade your iCloud Storage:* Select iCloud Storage in the sidebar, then click Upgrade to upgrade your iCloud storage plan, from 200 GB to 2 TB. Family members can share the

plan with you or keep their own individual storage plans.

- *Set up Location Sharing:* Select Location Sharing in the sidebar, then click Learn More to learn how to set up location sharing on all your devices. You can set up location sharing so that all family members can view each other's locations in the Find My app and Messages. You can use the Find My app on your Mac, iCloud.com, iOS and iPadOS devices.
- *Screen Time:* Select Screen Time in the sidebar, click Open Screen Time Settings, then select the options you want.
- *Subscribe to Apple Music:* Select Apple Music in the sidebar. If you don't have an Apple Music Family plan subscription, you can subscribe for a free 14-day trial. When you subscribe to an Apple Music family membership, all family members get unlimited access to Apple Music automatically.
- *Subscribe to TV Channels:* Select TV Channels in the sidebar. If you don't have a TV channel subscription, click Learn More to learn about TV channel subscriptions. When a family

member subscribes, all family members get unlimited access to TV Channels automatically.

- *Subscribe to Apple News+:* Select Apple News+ in the sidebar. If you don't have Apple News+ subscription, click Learn More to learn about Apple News+ subscriptions. When a family member subscribes, all family members get unlimited access to Apple News+ automatically.
- *Subscribe to Apple Arcade (not available in all countries or regions):* Select Apple Arcade in the sidebar. If you don't have an Apple Arcade subscription, click Learn More to learn about Apple Arcade subscriptions. When a family member subscribes, all family members get unlimited access to Apple Arcade automatically.

Before purchases are available to all family members, each person must confirm the Apple ID they use to share the iTunes Store, the App Store, and Apple Books purchases.

Set up Screen Time for a child on Mac

The most flexible and convenient way to set up and manage Screen Time for a child is by using Family Sharing. When you use Family Sharing, you can remotely manage and monitor each child's device usage from your own account on any Mac, iPhone, or iPad. However, if you aren't using Family Sharing, you can still set up Screen Time for a child by logging in to their Mac account.

1. On your Mac, do one of the following:
    - *If you're using Family Sharing:* Log in to your account, then make sure you're signed in with your Apple ID.
    - *If you aren't using Family Sharing:* Log in to the child's account.
2. Choose Apple menu > System Preferences, then click Screen Time.

3. If you're using Family Sharing, click the pop-up menu in the sidebar, then choose a child.
4. Click Options in the lower-left corner of the sidebar.
5. Click Turn On in the upper-right corner.
6. Select any of the following options:
    - *Include Website Data:* Select this option if you want Screen Time reports to include details about the specific websites visited. If you don't select this option, websites are just reported as Safari usage.
    - *Use Screen Time Passcode:* Select this option to keep Screen Time settings from being changed, and to require a passcode to allow additional time when limits expire.
7. If you want to, do any of the following:
    - Click Downtime in the sidebar, then set up a downtime schedule.
    - Click App Limits in the sidebar, then set time limits for apps and websites.
    - Click Always Allowed in the sidebar, then choose apps that can be used at any time.
    - Click Content & Privacy in the sidebar, then set up content & privacy restrictions.

Share purchases with others in your Family Sharing group

As a family member, you have immediate access to purchases that other family members share with each other. You can download their purchases on your computer, and iOS and iPadOS devices at any time. You can let other family members access your purchases in the same way. You can hide individual purchases you don't want other family members to share.

Before you can share family purchases, you must join a family and set up Purchase Sharing.

View and download purchases made by other family members

1. Go to the Purchased section in Music, the App Store, or Apple Books.
   - *In Music:* Choose Account > Purchased. If you don't see that menu command, choose Account > Sign In.
   - *In App Store:* Choose Store > View My Account.
   - *In Books:* Choose Store > Book Store Home, then click Purchased below Quick Links on the right.

2. Click your name or choose a family member to view their purchases.
3. Download the items you want.

When a family member initiates a purchase, it's billed directly to the family organizer's account. Once purchased, the item is added to the initiating family member's account and is shared with the rest of the family. If the family organizer ever stops Family Sharing, each person keeps the items they chose to purchase—even if they were paid for by the family organizer.

Hide a purchase from other family members

You can hide your individual Music, App Store, and Apple Books purchases so they aren't available to other family members.

1. Go to the Purchased section of Music, the App Store, or Apple Books.
   - *In Music:* Choose Account > Purchased. If you don't see that menu command, choose Account > Sign In.
   - *In App Store:* Choose Store > View My Account.

- *In Books:* Choose Store > Book Store Home, then click Purchased below Quick Links on the right.

2. Do one of the following:

- *In Music:* Select the type of content you want to hide, place the pointer over the item you want to hide, then click its Remove button .
- *In App Store:* Position the pointer over the item you want to hide, click , and then choose Hide Purchase.
- *In Books:* Place the pointer over the item you want to hide, then click its Remove button .

Stop hiding a purchase

You can reveal individual Music, App Store, and Apple Books purchases that you have hidden so that they are available to other family members.

1. Go to the Account Information section in Music, the App Store, or Apple Books.

- *In Music:* Choose Account > View My Account. If you don't see that menu command, choose Account > Sign In.
- *In App Store:* Choose Store > View My Account. If you don't see that menu command, choose Store > Sign In.
- *In Books:* Choose Store > View My Apple ID. If you don't see that menu command, choose Store > Sign In.

2. Do one of the following:
   - *In Music:* Scroll to Hidden Purchases, click Manage, and then click Unhide for the item.
   - *In App Store:* Click View information. In the hidden items section, click Manage, then click Unhide for the item.
   - *In Books:* Scroll to Hidden Purchases, click Manage, and then click Unhide for the item.

Stop sharing your purchases

1. On your Mac, choose Apple menu > System Preferences, click Family Sharing, then select Purchase Sharing in the sidebar.
2. Deselect Share My Purchases under your Account information.

Note: To share purchases, family members must be in the same iTunes Store country or region. If a family member changes their iTunes Store country or region, that person might lose access to other family members' purchases, and installed apps that were shared from other family members might not work.

Ways to share calendars on Mac

Share your calendar with friends and family

Share iCloud calendars with others who also have iCloud accounts. You can choose whether others can edit the calendar or only view it.

Share your calendar with coworkers

Share individual calendars or share calendar accounts with people who use the same calendar service. For example, if you share an Exchange or CalDAV server at work, you can choose whether coworkers can edit your calendar account or only view it.

Share a read-only version of your calendar with anyone

Publish a calendar to a web server or at a specific web address. Others can view the calendar on the web and subscribe to it using Calendar. Subscribers can view your calendar but they can't edit it.

Stop sharing a calendar

You can stop sharing or publishing any of your calendars. See the topics linked above.

Share a reminder list on Mac

You can share reminder lists in your upgraded iCloud reminders account with other iCloud users who've also upgraded their reminders. Everyone who shares the list can create and edit reminders from any computer or device set up with iCloud. Notifications aren't shared; you can set a reminder to remind you at a time or place, but it won't remind anyone else.

After you start sharing a reminder list, you can add or remove people, or stop sharing the list with anyone.

Note: All Reminders features described in this guide are available when using upgraded iCloud reminders. Some features aren't available when using accounts from other providers.

Share a list

1. In the Reminders app  on your Mac, choose View > Show Sidebar.
2. Select a reminder list in the sidebar, then click the Share button .

3. In the Add People window, choose how you'd like to send your invitation:
    - *Send invitation using Mail or Messages:* Click Mail or Messages, click Share, enter the people you want to share the list with, then click Send.
    - *Send invitation using a link or AirDrop:* Click Copy Link or AirDrop, enter addresses or phone numbers of the people you want to share the list with, then click Share.

The invitee must accept the invitation in order to view and edit the shared list.

Add people to a shared list

After you start sharing a reminder list, you can add more people who can see the list.

1. In the Reminders app on your Mac, choose View > Show Sidebar.
2. Select a reminder list in the sidebar, then click the Share button.
3. In the People window, click Add People.
4. In the Add People window, choose how you'd like to send your invitation:

- *Send invitation using Mail or Messages:* Click Mail or Messages, click Share, enter the people you want to share the list with, then click Send.
- *Send invitation using a link or Airdrop:* Click Copy Link or Airdrop, enter addresses or phone numbers of the people you want to share the list with, then click Share.

Remove people from a shared list

If you no longer want to share a list with a person, you can remove them from the shared list.

1. In the Reminders app on your Mac, choose View > Show Sidebar.
2. Select a reminder list in the sidebar, then click the Share button.
3. In the People window, select the person you want to remove.
4. Click the More Options button at the right, then choose Remove Access.
5. Click Done.

When you remove a person from the shared list, the list is removed from all of the other person's devices.

Stop sharing a list

If you change your mind about sharing a list or no longer need to share it, you can stop sharing it with everyone.

1. In the Reminders app on your Mac, choose View > Show Sidebar.
2. Select a reminder list in the sidebar, then click the Share button.
3. In the People window, click Stop Sharing, then click Continue.

When you stop sharing a list, the list is removed from all participants' devices.

Create a shared album in Photos on Mac

After you turn on Shared Albums, it's easy to create a shared album to share your photos and video clips.

Create a shared album

1. In the Photos app on your Mac, select the photos and video clips you want to share.
2. Click the Share button in the toolbar and choose Shared Albums, then click New Shared Album.

3. Type a name for the shared album, then type the email addresses of the people you want to share the album with.

   If you want subscribers to be able to view the shared album from an iPhone or iPad, be sure to use the email addresses they use to sign in with their Apple ID.

4. Click Create.

Your invitees are sent an email asking them to subscribe to your shared album.

View a shared album

1. In the Photos app on your Mac, click a shared album under Shared in the sidebar.

   You can also click Shared in the sidebar to see all your shared albums in the window, then double-click a shared album to view it.

2. Click < to see all your shared albums again.

Stop sharing an album

You can stop sharing an album with specific people by removing them from the subscribers list. To stop sharing a photo album entirely, you can delete it.

WARNING: When you delete a shared album, it's immediately removed from your devices and your subscribers' devices. If you think your subscribers might want to keep any photos or video from the album, you should alert them to save the items before you delete the shared album. Also, make sure you've downloaded any photos and videos that others have added to the album and that you want to keep. The photos you shared aren't deleted from your Photos library.

In the Photos app on your Mac, do one of the following:

- Click a shared album in the sidebar, click in the toolbar, and then click Delete Shared Album.
- Control-click the shared album you want to stop sharing, then choose Delete Shared Album.

View activity in your shared albums

To see the latest activity in your shared albums—including photos that have been recently added and who added them—use the Activity album, in your shared albums.

- In the Photos app  on your Mac, click Activity below Shared in the sidebar, then scroll to view changes.

Locate a friend in Find My on Mac

After you start following a friend, you can see and label their locations, contact them through Messages, FaceTime, or email, and get directions to where they are.

Ask Siri. Say something like: "Where's John Bishop?" In the Find My app  on your Mac, click People.

1. In the People list, select a name.
    - *If your friend can be located:* They appear on a map so you can see where they are.
    - *If your friend can't be located:* You see "No location found" below their name.

- *If you aren't following your friend:* You see "Can see your location" below their name. Ask to follow a friend to see their location.

2. Click the Info button on the map, then do any of the following:

   - *Label a friend's location:* Click Edit Location Name, then select an option (such as Home or Gym), or click Add Custom Label, enter a name, then press Return.

     The label appears below your friend's name instead of the location information.

   - *Contact a friend:* Click Contact, then choose an option.

   - *Get directions to a friend's location:* Click Directions.

     The Maps app opens with the directions from your location to your friend's location.

   - *Set up notifications*

Chapter 7

Use Your Apple Devices together

Use Continuity to work across Apple devices

With Continuity, you can use a variety of features that let your Mac and other Apple devices that support Continuity—like iPhone, iPad, iPod touch, and Apple Watch—work together in even smarter ways and let you seamlessly move between your devices.

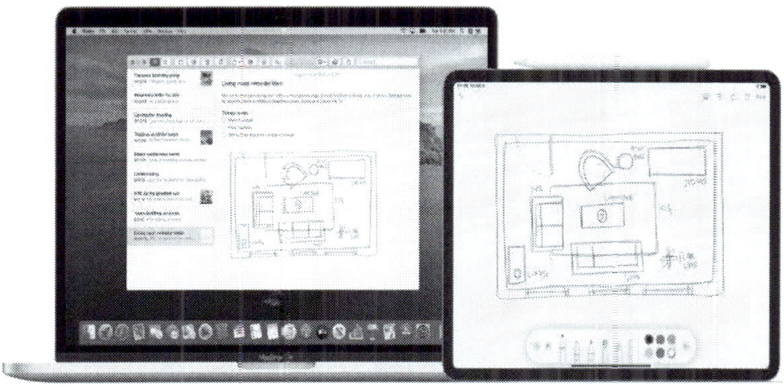

To use Continuity features, your devices must meet system requirements. See the Apple Support article System requirements for Continuity on Mac, iPhone, iPad, iPod touch, and Apple Watch.

Sidecar

When you use your iPad as a second display, you can have your iPad show the same apps and windows as your Mac, or extend your workspace by showing different apps and windows.

Handoff

Start a document, an email, or a message on one device and pick up where you left off on another device. Handoff works with apps like Mail, Safari, Maps, Messages, Reminders, Calendar, Contacts, Pages, Numbers, and Keynote.

Continuity Camera

Take a picture or scan a document with your nearby iPhone or iPad and have it appear instantly on your Mac..

Continuity Markup

Edit a PDF document or image on your Mac and see it on your nearby iPhone or iPad, where you can write and sketch on it using Markup tools—and Apple Pencil on iPad—and instantly see the changes on your Mac.

Continuity Sketch

Draw a sketch using your nearby iPhone or iPad and have the sketch appear instantly on your Mac.

Universal Clipboard

Copy text, images, photos, and videos on one Apple device and then paste the content on another Apple device. For example, you can copy a recipe from Safari on your Mac, then paste it into Notes on your nearby iPhone.

Auto Unlock and Approve with Apple Watch

Use your Apple Watch to unlock your Mac or approve authentication requests from your Mac, without having to enter a password.

Phone Calls

When you want to make or answer a phone call, don't reach for your iPhone—use your Mac. You can start calls from FaceTime, Contacts, Safari, Mail, Maps, Spotlight, and many other apps. When someone calls you, a notification appears. Just click the notification to answer.

SMS Messages

Send and receive SMS and MMS text messages right from your Mac. When friends text you, regardless of what phone they have, you can respond from whichever device is closest. All the messages that appear on your iPhone now appear on your Mac, too.

AirDrop

AirDrop lets you quickly share photos, videos, contacts, and anything else, with anyone near you—wirelessly. It makes sharing to iPhone, iPad, iPod touch, and Mac as simple as dragging and dropping.

Instant Hotspot

No Wi-Fi? No problem. Your Mac can connect to the internet using the personal hotspot on your iPhone or iPad when they're within range of each other. No setup is required. Your iPhone or iPad automatically appears in the Wi-Fi menu on your Mac—just select it to turn on your hotspot.

Use your iPad as a second display for your Mac

With Sidecar, you can use your iPad in landscape orientation as a second display for your Mac. Like any second display, you can extend your desktop by showing different apps or windows on your iPad, or instead make it show the same ones you see on your Mac.

Note: Sidecar is a Continuity feature. To use Continuity features, your devices must meet system requirements. See the Apple Support article System requirements for Continuity on Mac, iPhone, iPad, iPod touch, and Apple Watch.

Set Sidecar options

Make sure you're signed in with the same Apple ID on your Mac and iPad.

1. On your Mac, choose Apple menu > System Preferences, then click Sidecar.
2. Set options for showing the Sidebar and the Touch Bar on iPad, and for using Apple Pencil.
3. If you're not already connected to your iPad, click the "Connect to" pop-up menu, then choose your iPad.

   You can also connect from the Airplay menu in the menu bar or, in Displays preferences, from the AirPlay Display pop-up menu.

   You don't need to connect your iPad to your Mac with a cable to use Sidecar.

Use Sidecar

1. If you're not already connected to your iPad, click the Airplay menu in the menu bar on your Mac, then select your iPad.

   The Sidecar menu appears in the menu bar. You can easily change how you work with iPad from the Sidecar menu at any time. For example, switch between using iPad as a mirrored or separate display, or show or hide the Sidebar or Touch Bar on iPad.

2. Do any of the following:

    - *Move windows from Mac to iPad:* Drag a window to the edge of the screen until the pointer appears on your iPad. Or while using an app, choose Window > Move Window to iPad.

    - *Move windows from iPad to Mac:* Drag a window to the edge of the screen until the pointer appears on your Mac. Or while using an app, choose Window > Move Window Back to Mac.

    - *Use the Sidebar on iPad:* With your finger or Apple Pencil, tap icons in the Sidebar to show or hide the menu bar when you're using an app full screen, the Dock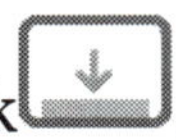, or the keyboard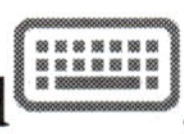. Or tap one or more modifier keys, such as Ctrl, to use keyboard shortcuts.

    - *Use the Touch Bar on iPad:* With your finger or Apple Pencil, tap any button in the Touch

Bar. The buttons available vary depending on the app or task.

- *Use Apple Pencil on iPad:* With your Apple Pencil, tap to select items such as menu commands, checkboxes, or files. If your Apple Pencil supports it (and you set the option in Sidecar preferences), you can double-tap the lower section of your Apple Pencil to switch drawing tools in some apps.
- *Use gestures on iPad:* Use basic gestures, such as tap, swipe, scroll, and zoom, as well as gestures for entering and editing text. *Switch between the Mac desktop and the iPad on iPad:* Swipe up from the bottom edge of your iPad with one finger to show the iPad Home screen. To show the iPad Dock, swipe up and pause. To show the iPad App Switcher, swipe up and pause in the center of the screen. To return to the Mac desktop, swipe up, then tap the Sidecar icon .

3. When you're ready to stop using your iPad, click the Disconnect icon  at the bottom of the Sidebar on iPad.

You can also disconnect from the Sidecar menu in the menu bar or in Sidecar or Displays system preferences.

Pick up where you left off with Handoff on Mac

With Handoff, you can start something on one device (Mac, iPhone, iPad, or Apple Watch) and then pick it up on another without losing focus on what you're doing. For example, look at a webpage on your iPhone, then pick up where you left off in Safari on your Mac. You can use Handoff with many Apple apps—for example, Calendar, Contacts, Pages, or Safari. Some third-party apps may also work with Handoff.

To use Handoff, your devices must meet Continuitysystem requirements. They must also have Wi-Fi, Bluetooth, and Handoff turned on in System Preferences (on your Mac) and in Settings (on your iOS and iPadOS devices). You must be signed in with the same Apple ID on all your devices.

Tip: When Handoff is on, you can use Universal Clipboard to copy and paste text, images, photos, and videos across devices. You can also copy files between Mac computers.

Turn Handoff on or off

Note: If you don't see a Handoff option on your device, it doesn't work with Handoff.

- *On your Mac:* Choose Apple menu > System Preferences, click General, then select "Allow Handoff between this Mac and your iCloud devices" (below "Recent items"). To turn it off, deselect the option.
- *On iPad, iPhone, or iPod touch:* Go to Settings > General > Handoff, then tap to turn on Handoff. To turn it off, tap the option.
- *On Apple Watch:* Open the Watch app on iPhone, go to My Watch > General, then tap to turn on Enable Handoff. To turn it off, tap the option.

Hand off between devices

- *From your Mac to an iOS or iPadOS device:* The Handoff icon of the app you're using on your Mac appears on your iPhone (at the bottom of the app switcher) or your iPad or iPod touch (at the end of the Dock). Tap to continue working in the app.
- *From an iOS or iPadOS device or Apple Watch to your Mac:* The Handoff icon of the app you're using

on your iPhone, iPad, iPod touch, or Apple Watch appears on your Mac at the left end of the Dock (or the top, depending on the Dock position). Click the icon to continue working in the app.

You can also press Command-Tab to quickly switch to the app that has the Handoff icon.

Insert photos and scans with Continuity Camera on Mac

With Continuity Camera, you can take a picture or scan a form or document using your nearby iPhone or iPad and have the photo or scan appear instantly on your Mac, exactly where you need it—for example, in an email, a message, a document, a note, or a folder.

To use Continuity features, your devices must meet system requirements.

1. On your Mac, position the cursor where you want to insert a photo or scan.

For example, in a document, a note, an email, or a text.

2. Choose File > Import from iPhone or iPad, then choose Take Photo or Scan Documents.

   You can also Control-Click the desktop or a folder in a Finder window, choose Import from iPhone or iPad, then choose Take Photo or Scan Documents.

   If you don't see the commands in the File menu, they may be in another menu (such as the Edit or Insert menu) or the app you're using might not support Continuity Camera.

3. On your iPhone or iPad, do one of the following:

   - *For a photo:* Take the photo, then tap Use Photo or Retake.
   - *For a scan:* Take the scan. Your device detects the edges of the document and autocorrects any skewing of the image—if you want to adjust the area included in the scan, drag the frame or its edges. When you're ready, tap Keep Scan or Retake. When you have the scan you want, tap Save.

4. On your Mac, the picture or scan appears where you positioned the cursor.

Depending on where the photo or scan is inserted, you can mark it up or adjust other aspects, such as crop it or apply a filter.

Scans you take on your iOS or iPadOS device are not saved on the device.

Insert sketches with Continuity Sketch on Mac

You can draw a sketch using your nearby iPhone or iPad and have the sketch appear instantly on your Mac, exactly where you need it—for example, in an email, a message, a document, a note, or a folder.

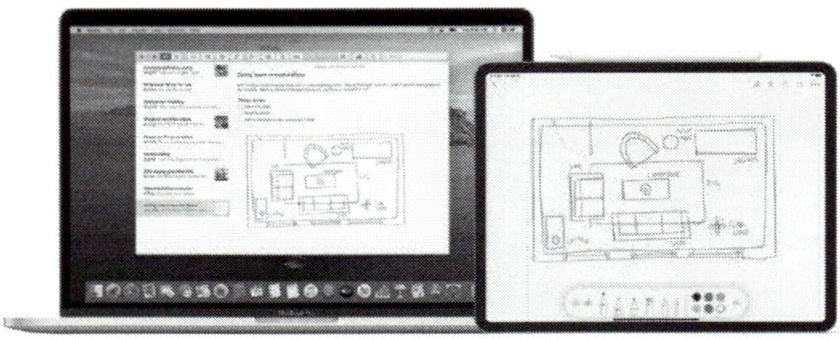

To use Continuity features, your devices must meet system requirements. On your Mac, position the cursor where you want to insert a sketch or markup.

For example, in a document, a note, or an email.

1. Choose File > Import from iPhone or iPad, then choose Add Sketch.

   You can also Control-Click the desktop or a folder in a Finder window, choose Import from iPhone or iPad, then choose Add Sketch.

If you don't see the commands in the File menu, they may be in another menu (such as the Edit or Insert menu) or the app you're using might not support them.

2. On your iPhone or iPad, draw a sketch using your finger; on iPad, you can also use Apple Pencil.
3. When you're ready, tap done.
4. On your Mac, the sketch appears where you positioned the cursor or, if you started from the desktop, as a file to save.

   Depending on where the sketch is inserted, you can mark it upor adjust other aspects, such as apply a filter or change its size.

Copy and paste between devices from your Mac

With Universal Clipboard, you can copy text, images, photos, and videos on one Apple device and then paste the content on another Apple device. For example, you can copy a recipe from your Mac and paste it into a note on your nearby iPhone. Or copy a file from one Mac to paste in a folder on another Mac.

- *Copy on a device:* Select the content you want to copy, then copy it. For example, on your Mac, press Command-C or choose Edit > Copy.

The copied content is available to paste on your other devices only for a short time.

- *Paste on a device:* Position the pointer where you want to paste the content, then paste it. For example, on your iPad, double tap, then choose Paste from the options.

Note: To use Universal Clipboard, your devices must meet Continuity system requirements. They must also have Wi-Fi, Bluetooth, and Handoff turned on in System Preferences (on your Mac) and in Settings (on your iOS and iPadOS devices). You must be signed in with the same Apple IDon all your devices.

Unlock your Mac and approve requests with Apple Watch

When you're wearing your Apple Watch, you can use it to unlock your Mac or approve app requests, without having to enter a password.

Note: To use these features, make sure you're signed in with the same Apple ID on your Mac (a mid-2013 or later model) and Apple Watch, two-factor authentication is turned on for your Apple ID, and your Apple Watch is unlocked.

Turn on Auto Unlock and Approve with Apple Watch

1. Choose Apple menu > System Preferences, then click Security & Privacy.
2. Click General, then select "Use your Apple Watch to unlock apps and your Mac" (available if your Apple Watch has watchOS 6 installed).

   If your Apple Watch has watchOS 3, 4, or 5 installed, select "Allow your Apple Watch to unlock your Mac." (You can't approve app requests.)

Before you can select an option, you may need to click the lock icon at the bottom of the pane, then type an administrator name and password.

Unlock your Mac

Wake your Mac from its idle state by pressing any keyboard key or, on a portable, by opening the display. The screen indicates your Mac is being unlocked.

Approve app requests

When an app requires authentication on your Mac—for example, to view passwords, unlock notes or preferences, and approve app installations—an approval request from your Mac appears on your Apple Watch.

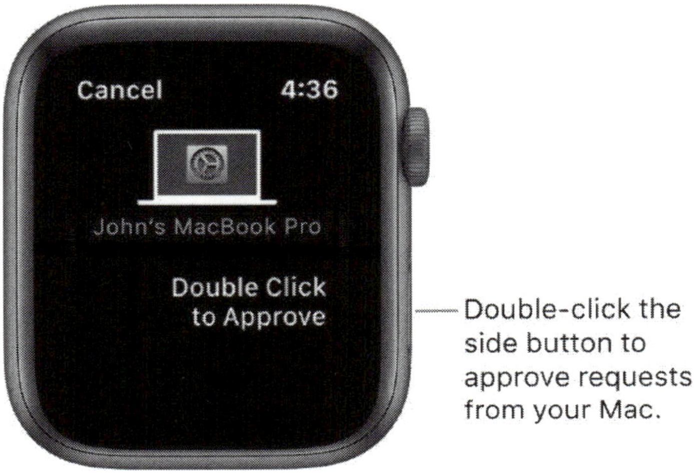

Double-click the side button of your Apple Watch to approve the task request.

If you're not sure your Mac supports Auto Unlock and Approve with Apple Watch, choose Apple menu > About This Mac, then click System Report. In the sidebar, click Network, click Wi-Fi, and then look on the right for "Auto Unlock: Supported."

If you're the administrator for another user on your Mac, you can log in to their user account and turn on Auto Unlock or Approve with Apple Watch for them, as long as their Apple ID uses two-factor authentication and their Apple Watch has the required watchOS installed.

Make and receive phone calls in FaceTime on Mac

When you want to make or receive a phone call, you don't have to reach for your iPhone—you can use your Mac. When someone calls you, a notification appears on your Mac and you can take the call—and even use Real-Time Text (RTT)for your phone calls, if your carrier supports it.

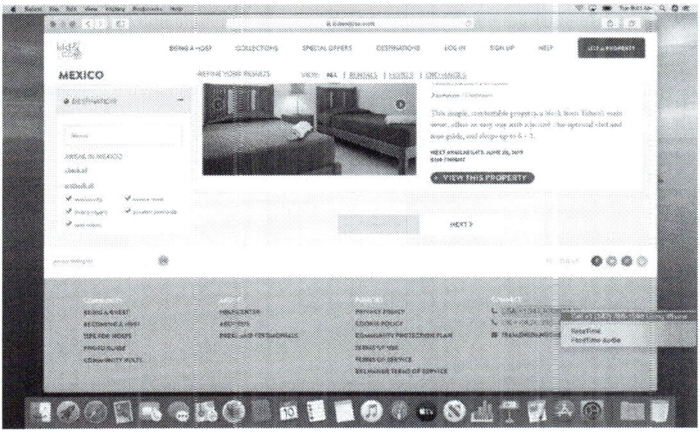

Note: Phone calls you make and receive on your Mac use cellular minutes—cellular charges may apply.

Make calls from apps on your Mac

1. In the FaceTime app on your Mac, sign in and turn on FaceTime.
2. Set up your iPhone and Mac for phone calls, if you haven't done so already.
3. In these apps on your Mac, do one of the following:

- *FaceTime:* Enter a phone number in the search field (you may need to press Return), then click the Audio button (or use the Touch Bar). You can also click Audio to see your past phone calls.

  If you enabled RTT phone calls, you can choose to make an RTT call.

- *Contacts:* Select a contact, move your pointer over a phone number, then click the Phone button.

  If you enabled RTT phone calls, you can choose to make an RTT call.

- *Safari:* Click a phone number on a webpage, then click Call.

- *Mail:* Place the pointer over a phone number in an email, click the pop-up menu, and then choose how you want to make the call.

- *Maps:* Click a place of interest, click the Info button, and then click Call.

- *Spotlight:* Enter the name of a person or place in the Spotlight search field, then select the matching search result. Move the pointer over a phone number, then click the Phone button.

- *Calendar:* Open an event, look for an underlined blue phone number in the event details, then click the number.
- *Reminders:* Open the reminders list, then click an underlined blue phone number. Or, move the pointer over a reminder, click the Info button, look for a phone number in the notes, then click the number.

Answer calls on your Mac

On your Mac, when a notification appears in the top-right corner of the screen, do one of the following:

- *Accept an incoming call:* Click Accept.

  If the person calling you has enabled RTT for the call and you want to answer it that way, click RTT.

- *Decline a call:* Click Decline.

  Tip: If the call came from someone you don't want to receive calls from, you can block the caller.

- *Decline a call and send a message using I Message:*

  Click next to Decline, choose Reply with Message,

type your message, and then click Send. Both you and the caller must be signed in to I Message.

- *Decline a call and set a reminder to call back later:*

  Click next to Decline, then choose how long you want to wait to receive a reminder. When the time comes, you receive a notification—click it to view the reminder, then click the link in the reminder to start the call.

If your Mac has a Touch Bar, you can use it to accept a call, decline a call, decline and send a message, or decline and set a reminder.

Manage calls on your Mac

While you're on a phone call in the FaceTime app on your Mac, there are a few additional ways to manage the call:

- *Switch to a FaceTime video call:* Click Video in the notification (or use the Touch Bar).
- *Switch to an RTT call:* Click RTT in the notification.

  Note: When you switch a phone call to an RTT call, the microphone remains active—click the Mute button (or use the Touch Bar) to turn off audio for the call.

- *Use call waiting:* If you're on a call, and a new phone call notification appears, click Hold & Accept. Click  to switch between calls.
- *Start a conference call when you have another call on hold:* When you're on a phone call and have another phone call on hold, click Merge.
- *Transfer the call to your iPhone:* When your Mac is near your iPhone, tap the Handoff icon that appears in the bottom-left corner of the Lock screen of your iPhone.

  Depending on how you set up Wi-Fi Calling, a green bar that says "Touch to return to call" might appear at the top of the screen on your iPhone when you unlock it.
- *Control the volume:* Mute or change the volume for the call.

Tip: If you're on a call and need to respond to prompts in an automated phone system, click the phone call notification in the top-right corner of your screen and use the numbers on your keyboard to respond.

Control Home accessories on Mac

You can control Home Kit accessories with the Home app on your Mac.

Control an accessory

- Click an accessory to turn it on or off, or double-click it to see more options. The available controls depend on the type of accessory. For example, with some lightbulbs you can change brightness or colors.

Control an accessory with multiple features

Accessories with multiple features are controlled by one accessory tile. For example, if you have a ceiling fan with a built-in light, you can control the speed of the fan and the brightness of the light from the same tile. Similarly, if you have a sensor that detects humidity, temperature, and air quality, all features are controlled from one tile.

The available controls depend on the type of accessory.

1. In the Home app on your Mac, double-click an accessory tile that has multiple features.
2. Click Accessories, then click one of the features to control or view it.

Control a thermostat

- You can control a thermostat by moving the selector on the Ring controller, or clicking on a mode, such as Heat, Cool, or Auto.

Add an accessory to a room

You can add an accessory to a room or move it to another room.

1. In the Home app on your Mac, click the Home button, double-click an accessory.
2. Click Room, choose a room from the list (or create a new room), then click in the top-right corner.

   Tip: Right-click (or Control-click) an accessory tile to quickly access the Show Controls and Settings buttons.

Rename an accessory

1. In the Home app on your Mac, click the Home button, double-click an accessory.
2. Delete the accessory's name, enter a new one, and then click in the top-right corner.

Edit a room

- In the Home app on your Mac, choose Edit > Edit Room. You can change the room's name or wallpaper, or you can remove the room.

  Tip: You can customize your wallpaper by dragging and dropping an image such as a JPG or TIFF file.

Add a room to a zone

You can group rooms to form a zone so that accessories in similar rooms are controlled at once. For example, you could create a zone to control all of the rooms on the ground floor of your house and call it downstairs.

1. In the Home app on your Mac, choose Edit > Edit Room.
2. Click Rooms in the top-left corner of the window, then click on a room.
3. Click Zone, click a zone from the list or click Create New to create a new one, then click done.

   Add two or more rooms to create a zone.

   To target this zone, say to Siri: "Turn off the downstairs lights." You can't rename a zone, but you can delete it by swiping left with two fingers on a trackpad and clicking Delete.

Make an accessory a favorite

By default, the first eight accessories you add to Home are automatically listed as favorites, but you can add more accessories as favorites.

1. In the Home app on your Mac, choose View in the menu bar, then choose the room to which the accessory is assigned.
2. Double-click the accessory, then click Include in Favorites.
3. Click in the top-right corner.

   The accessory appears as a favorite.

Change a lightbulb's icon

You can change the icon of a lightbulb; you can't change the icon of other accessories.

1. In the Home app on your Mac, click the Home button, double-click a lightbulb accessory.
2. Click the lightbulb icon, then choose an alternative.

   Click done, then click in the top-right corner.

Rearrange your favorites

1. In the Home app on your Mac, click the Home button or Rooms button.
2. Click and drag an accessory or scene to move it.

Use Airdrop on your Mac to send files to devices near you

Airdrop lets you wirelessly send documents, photos, webpages, and more to anyone nearby who's on the same Wi-Fi network. You can send items between Mac computers and iOS devices.

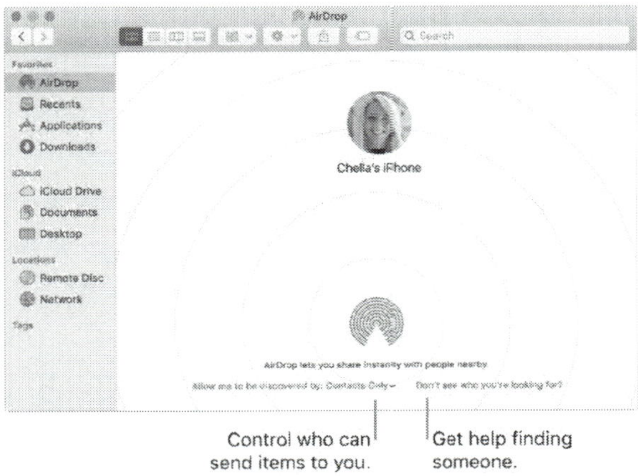

Send items using Airdrop

With Airdrop on your Mac, you can send items from the Finder, the desktop, or from within apps such as Safari or Maps.

- *From the desktop or a Finder window:* Control-click the item you want to send, choose Share >Airdrop from the shortcut menu, then select the device you want to send the item to.

- *From the Finder:* Click Airdrop in the Finder sidebar, then drag the item to the device you want to send it to.
- *From an app:* Click the Share button in the app's toolbar, choose Airdrop, and then select the device you want to send the item to.

If you don't see the person's device in the Airdrop window, click "Don't see who you're looking for?"

Receive items using Airdrop

When someone uses Airdrop to send an item to you on your Mac, you can choose whether to accept and save it.

If you send an item from one device to another (for example, from your iPhone to your Mac), and you're signed in to iCloud using the same Apple ID on both devices, the item is automatically accepted and saved.

1. In the Airdrop notification on your Mac, click the Accept pop-up menu, then choose an option.
2. Look for the item in your Downloads folder or the app you saved the item to.

If someone who wants to send you a file can't see your Mac, make sure you've set it up to allow others to send items to you using Airdrop.

Allow others to send items to your Mac using Airdrop

1. On your Mac, click the Finder icon in the Dock to open a Finder window.
2. In the Finder sidebar, click Airdrop.
3. In the Airdrop window, click the "Allow me to be discovered by" pop-up menu, then choose an option.

Airdrop uses Bluetooth and Wi-Fi to transfer items between devices. Most likely, you've already got Bluetooth and Wi-Fi enabled on your Mac. If you don't, you're asked to turn them on when you try to send an item.

Use Air Pods with your Mac

When your Air Pods are nearby and ready to use with your Mac, you can use them to listen to music, use Siri, or handle phone calls.

If you're Air Pods are connected with your iPhone

If you already connected your Air Pods with your iPhone, they're ready to use with your Mac (your Mac must support Handoff and you must be signed in to iCloud using the same Apple ID).

1. Open the Air Pods case.

2. Click the Volume control in the menu bar on your Mac, then choose Air Pods.

Connect your Air Pods with your Mac

If your Air Pods are not connected with your iPhone, you can connect them directly with your Mac.

1. With your Air Pods in their case, open the lid.
2. Press and hold the setup button on the back of the case until the status light flashes white.
3. On your Mac, choose Apple menu > System Preferences, then click Bluetooth.
4. Select Air Pods in the Devices list, then click Connect.

Tip: If your Air Pods support it, say "Hey Siri." If Siri doesn't respond, open Siri preferences and make sure Listen for "Hey Siri" on Air Pods is turned on.

Use Airplay to stream what's on your Mac to an HDTV

Airplay Mirroring lets you send what's on your Mac to an HDTV wirelessly with Apple TV. If your Mac supports Airplay Mirroring, an Airplay status icon appears in the menu bar of your Mac when an Apple TV is on the same network as your Mac.

1. Make sure your Mac and Apple TV are on the same network.

2. Click the Airplay status icon in the menu bar, then choose your Apple TV.

   Note: If you don't see the Airplay status icon in the menu bar, check that your Apple TV is set up correctly.

3. To set whether you're desktop matches the size of the Mac screen or the TV screen, click the Airplay status icon then choose This Mac or your Apple TV. When you're using Airplay Mirroring, the Airplay status icon in the menu bar is blue.

Chapter 8

Music, TV, Books, News and more

Play songs in Music on Mac

Listen to your music the way you like—use the controls in the Music window to repeat songs, change the order they play in, and more.

Ask Siri. Say something like:

- "Play some music."
- "What song is this?"

1. In the Music app  on your Mac, click any option under Library in the sidebar. For example, click Albums to see all the albums in your library.
2. Double-click a song to play it or click the Play button  (or use the Touch Bar).
3. Do any of the following:
    - Shuffle or repeat songs.
    - Use the Up Next list.
    - Play songs in a specific order.
    - Fade between songs.
    - Prevent a song from playing.
    - Love or dislike songs.

You can also listen to music from a CD

Watch Now in the Apple TV app

The Watch Now pane in the Apple TV app is the place to start watching movies and TV shows (not all content is available in all countries or regions). Find what you want to watch, add it to your Up Next list, and then start watching.

Browse content

1. Open the Apple TV app on your Mac.
2. Click Watch Now.

   The Up Next row displays content you've added to Up Next, including content you've started watching but haven't finished.
3. Scroll down to view recommended TV shows and movies—including collections hand-picked by experts as well as dedicated categories based on your viewing history.

4. Click an item to see its rating, description, available viewing options, and purchase or rental information.

Play a movie or TV show

When you find what you want to watch in the Apple TV app on your Mac, click it, then do any of the following:

- *Play the item:* Click Play. (The Play button is available for free content, content you've already purchased, or content on Apple TV channels you subscribe to.)
- *Subscribe to an Apple TV channel:* Click "Try [*channel*]" and follow the onscreen instructions.
- *Buy or rent a movie:* Click Buy or Rent, then select the option you want and confirm your purchase or rental. For details,

Buy a TV show episode or season: Click Buy, then select the option you want and confirm your purchase. For details,

See what's up next

The Up Next row displays content you've already started to watch or plan to watch.

- In the Watch Now pane of the Apple TV app on your Mac, scroll to the Up Next row to see shows you've recently watched or added to Up Next. To see additional items, move the pointer to the beginning or end of the row, then click the left or right arrow that appears.

Shows and movies appear in the order you're most likely to want to watch them. For example, when a TV episode is finished, the next episode automatically appears in Up Next. And if you've already caught up on a show, whenever a new episode becomes available, it immediately shows up in the beginning of the Up Next row.

If you have an iPhone, iPad, iPod touch, or Apple TV and are signed in with the same Apple ID you use for the Mac, your viewing progress and episode selection stay in sync in the Apple TV app on those devices. For example, you can start watching a show on your Mac and finish watching it on your iPad, or vice versa.

Add a movie or TV show to Up Next

1. In the Watch Now pane of the Apple TV app on your Mac, click an item to see its rating, description, available viewing options, and purchase or rental information.

2. Click Add to Up Next.

   The Add to Up Next button changes to In up Next, indicating that the item is added.

Remove an item from Up Next

- In the Watch Now pane of the Apple TV app on your Mac, click In up Next. (If you don't see the inupnext button, first click the item in the Up Next row.)

Start watching from Up Next

- In the Watch Now pane of the Apple TV app on your Mac, move the pointer over an item in the Up Next row, then click the Play button that appears.

  If the item is not available to play immediately, follow the onscreen instructions.

Click the Close button to return to Watch Now

Listen to podcasts on Mac

Podcasts are free audio shows that you can stream and play on your Mac. You can listen to individual episodes, or you can subscribe to a show so that new episodes are automatically downloaded as they become available.

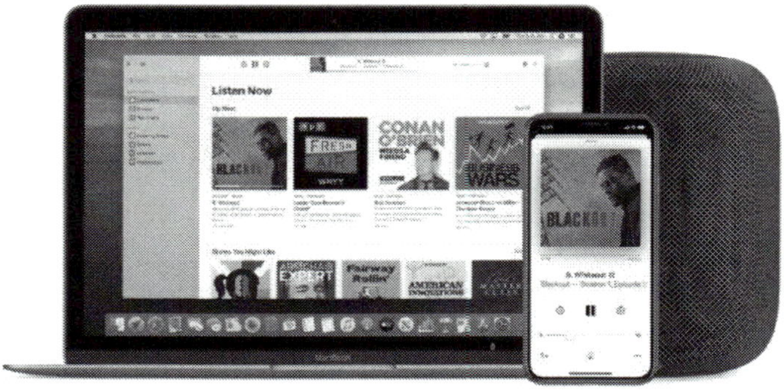

Your podcast subscriptions, stations, and current play position sync to the Podcasts app on all your devices when you sign in with the same Apple ID.

Listen to an episode

1. In the Podcasts app on your Mac, click Listen Now (or any item) in the sidebar.
2. Hold the pointer over the show or episode you want to play, then click the Play button .

   When the episode plays, you see the playback controls at the top of the Podcasts window.

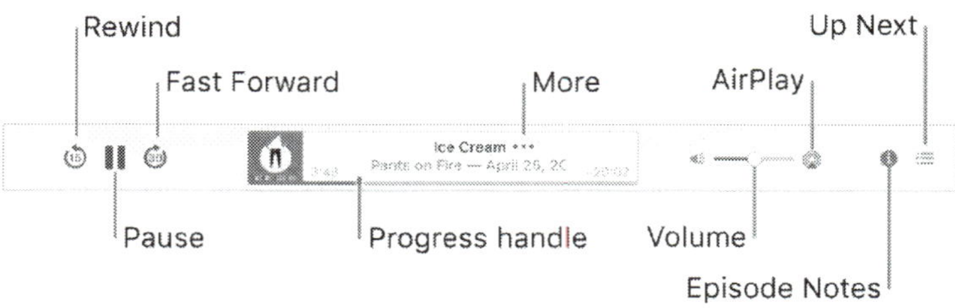

3. Do any of the following with the playback controls:

- *Skip ahead or skip back within the episode:* Drag the progress handle right (to skip ahead) or left (to skip back), or use the Touch Bar.

  You can also use the Skip Back button to go back (in 15-second increments) and the Skip Forward button to skip ahead (in 30-second increments) in the episode.

  Tip: You can customize the amount of time an episode goes back or skips ahead.

- *Pause the episode:* Click the Pause button (or use the Touch Bar).

  Click the Play button to resume playback (or use the Touch Bar).

- *Change the playback speed:* Choose Controls > Playback Speed, then choose a speed.
- *Change the audio output:* Click the Airplay button to choose which speakersto use to listen to the podcast.
- *Manage the episode (for example, copy the link, share the episode, or go to the Show page):* Hold the pointer over the episode

playing, click the morebutton , and then choose an option.

Note: If you've added the episode to the library, you can do even more to manage the episode—add it to the Up Next list, save it, and more.

- *Read the episode description:* Click the Episode Notes button .

Ask Siri. Say something like:

- "Forward 15 seconds."
- "Continue playing the last podcast."

Use the Up Next list

While listening to podcasts, you can use the Up Next list to view and change which episodes (or chapters within an episode) play next.

1. In the Podcasts app on your Mac, click any option in the sidebar.
2. Hold the pointer over a show or episode, click the morebutton , and then choose Play Next or Play Later.

The show or episode is added to the Up Next list (also known as the *queue*) at the top of the list (if you choose Play Next) or the bottom of the list (if you choose Play Later).

3. Click the Up Next button, then do any of the following:

   - *Play an episode (or chapter within an episode) in the list:* Click the episode or chapter.

     Note: Some podcasts include chapters within an episode, which allow you to jump quickly to a specific part of the episode.

   - *Change the order of episodes you manually added to Up Next:* Drag episodes with the Reorder button into the order you want.

The Up Next list appears onscreen until you click the Up Next button again to close it.

To control other aspects of playback, including whether to continue playing the next episode or what action is taken when you use headphone controls.

Read books in Books on Mac

Once you get books from the Book Store or download books you purchased on other devices, you can start reading and enjoying them.

If you'd rather have a book read to you, you might enjoy listening to audiobooks.

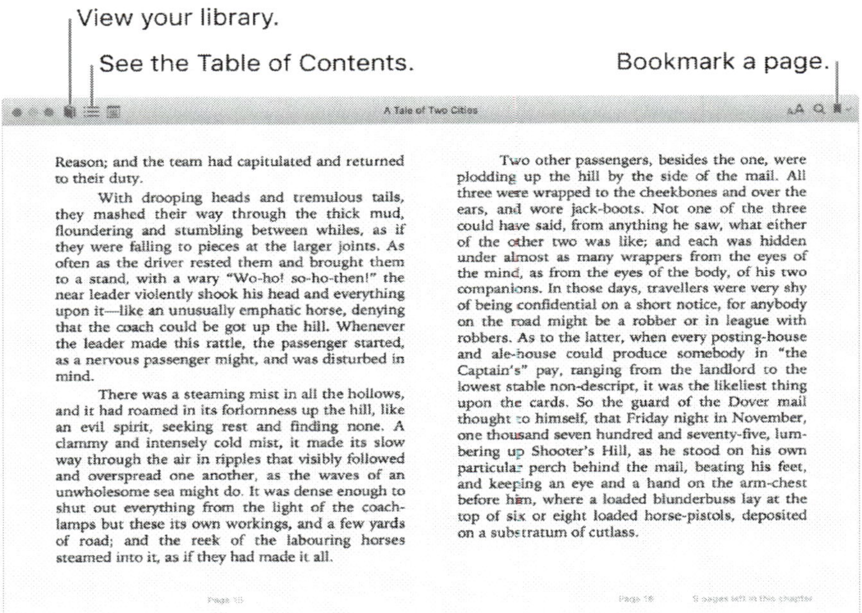

Open and move around in a book

1. In the Books app on your Mac, click Library in the toolbar, then double-click a book.

   Note: If the book has an iCloud status icon, it's downloaded from iCloud when you double-click it (you might need to sign in first).

2. Move around the book:

   - *See the table of contents:* Move the pointer to the top of the book, then click the Table of Contents button or the Thumbnails button, depending on the book.
   - *Go to the next or previous page:* Move the pointer to the right or left edge of the book, then click the arrow that appears.

     You can also swipe right or left across a trackpad or Magic Mouse, use the Touch Bar, or use the arrow keys on the keyboard. See Use trackpad and mouse gestures.
   - *See pages you already viewed:* Click the "Back to page" link at the bottom-left corner of the page (or use the Touch Bar). This is useful if you're viewing search results or different sections in the book's table of contents.

     You can always click the "Go to page" link in the bottom-right corner to return to the page you started on.

Save your place with a bookmark

1. In the Books app on your Mac, click Library in the toolbar, then double-click a book.
2. On the page you want to bookmark, move the pointer to the top of the page, then click the Bookmark button (or use the Touch Bar).

   If the page is already bookmarked, the Bookmark button is red.

To see all the bookmarks in a book, click the arrow next to the Bookmark button. If you want to delete a bookmark, move the pointer over it, then click ✕.

Have a book read to you

1. In the Books app on your Mac, click Library in the toolbar, then double-click a book.
2. Do one of the following:
   - *For books that include the Read Aloud feature:*

     Click the Speaker button in the toolbar at the top of the book, then click Start Reading (or use the Touch Bar).
   - *For any book:* Go to the page you want, then choose Edit > Speech > Start Speaking

Add, remove, or reorder ticker symbols in Stocks on Mac

Customize the watch list to display the ticker symbols you view regularly.

You don't need to know a specific ticker symbol to add it to your list. Just knowing the name is enough to get you started.

Add ticker symbols to your watch list

1. In the Stocks app on your Mac, type a name or ticker symbol in the search field.
2. In the search results list, click the ticker symbol you want to add.

   Detailed information about the ticker symbol is displayed in the pane on the right.
3. In the pane on the right, click the Add to watch list button near the upper right.

To clear the search field and return to your watch list, click the Delete button in the search field.

Remove ticker symbols from your watch list

- In the Stocks app on your Mac, Control-click a ticker symbol in the watch list, then choose Remove from Watch list.

Reorder ticker symbols in your watch list

- In the Stocks app on your Mac, select a ticker symbol in the watch list, then drag it to another position in the list.

Pay with Apple Pay in Safari on Mac

You can easily and securely shop on your Mac in Safari using Apple Pay. Look for Apple Pay when you check out, then complete your purchase using your Mac with Touch ID, iPhone (iOS 10 or later), or Apple Watch (watchOS 3 or later). If you complete your purchase using iPhone or Apple Watch, you must be signed in with the same Apple IDas on your Mac.

Note: Apple Pay is not available in all areas.

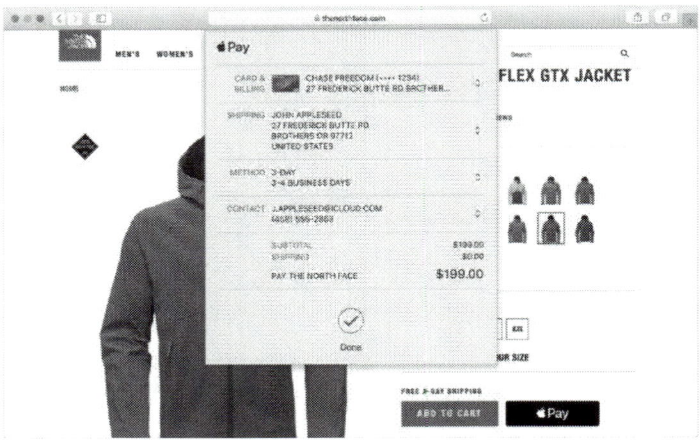

Before using Apple Pay, set up your credit or debit card on the device you'll use to complete your purchase.

1. In the Safari app on your Mac, at checkout, click Apple Pay.

   You can change the credit card, shipping address, or contact information before completing your purchase.

2. Complete the purchase.

   - *Mac with Touch ID:* Use Touch ID.

     Only one user account on your Mac can use Touch ID on the Mac to complete purchases with Apple Pay. Other user accounts must use iPhone or Apple Watch.

   - *IPhone:* Double-click the side button, then authenticate with Face IDon iPhone X; or use Touch ID on other models.

   - *Apple Watch:* Double-click the side button.

Record a voice memo on your Mac

With Voice Memos, use your Mac as a recording device. To record voice memos on Mac, use the built-in microphone, a supported headset, or an external mic. You can listen to your voice memos on any device where you're signed in using the same Apple ID and Voice Memos is turned on in iCloud preferences.

1. In the Voice Memos app on your Mac, choose File > Start New Recording or click the Record button .

2. To pause, click the Pause button . To continue, click Resume.

3. When you finish, click done in the lower-right corner.

Your recording is saved with the name of your location (if "Location-based naming" is selected in preferences) or with the name "New Recording."

After a recording is saved, you can select it to play or make edits, such as renaming or trimming.

Sync content between your Mac and iPhone or iPad

The first time you set up syncing, you must connect your device to your Mac using a USB or USB-C cable. After you connect the device, the device icon appears in the Finder sidebar and selecting the icon displays syncing options. You then select which items to sync.

You can sync all items of a specific type (which is the quickest option), or select specific items to sync (which gives you more control)—or you can do both. For example you can sync all of your music to your device, but sync only a selection of specific movies.

After you select what to sync, your Mac syncs items to your device automatically each time you connect your device.

If you have an iPhone (with iOS 5 or later) or iPad, you can also set up to sync wirelessly when your Mac and device are connected to the same Wi-Fi network. To learn how to turn on wireless syncing, for more information about syncing,

Automatically sync all items of a content type

1. Connect your device to your Mac.

   You can connect your device using a USB or USB-C cable or using a Wi-Fi connection. To turn on Wi-Fi syncing,

2. In the Finder on your Mac, select the device in the Finder sidebar.

3. Select a type of content you want to sync in the button bar.

Note: If you use iCloud Photos and Apple Music, your photos and music are synced automatically via iCloud. When you click Music or Photos, no options appear for syncing.

4. Select the "Sync [*content type*] onto [*device name*]" checkbox to turn on syncing for that type of item. For example, select the "Sync movies onto [*device name*]" checkbox to sync your movies.

With the checkbox selected, syncing is set to transfer all items of that type to your device.

5. Repeat steps 3 and 4 for each type of content you want to sync.

The bar at the bottom of the window shows how much free space remains on your device after you sync. Move the pointer over the bar to view details about the content you're syncing.

6. When you're ready to sync, click Apply.

By default, your Mac syncs your device whenever you connect it. To confirm that you want to sync whenever you connect, select General in the button bar, then deselect "Automatically sync when this [*device*] is connected."

WARNING: If you delete an automatically synced item from your Mac, the deleted item is removed from your device the next time you sync.

Before disconnecting your device from your Mac, click the Eject button in the Finder sidebar.

Play games on your Mac

It's easy to play games on your Mac. When you sign in with your Apple ID, a Game Center account is created for you (if it didn't exist already).

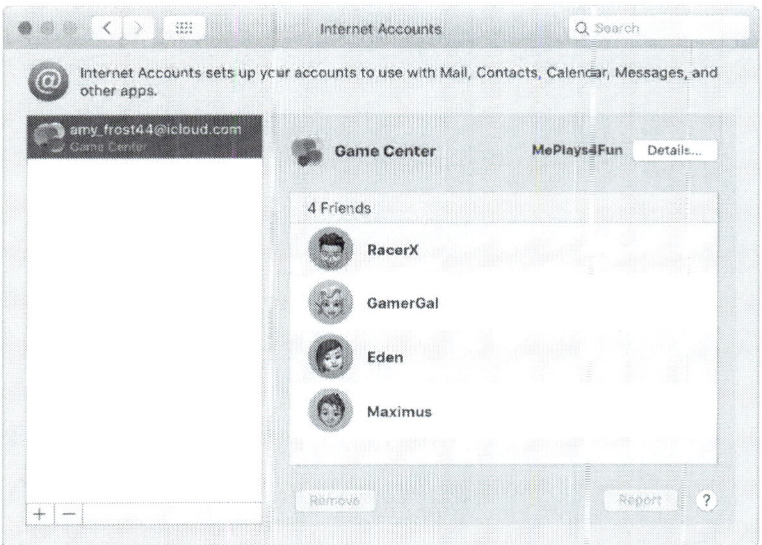

To play, open a game the same way you open any app on your Mac, then have fun. You can play alone in a single player game or play with others in a multiplayer game (real-time or turn-based). If a multiplayer game supports *sessions*, where the game data is stored in iCloud, you and your friends can come and go in the game whenever you want.

Tip: Browse the Mac App Store to get the newest or most popular games that support Game Center.

Customize your Game Center account

1. On your Mac, choose Apple menu > System Preferences, then click Internet Accounts.

   If you don't see a Game Center account in the sidebar, you can add it. Scroll to the bottom of the pane on the right, click Add Other Account, scroll down and click "Game Center account," then sign in.
2. In your Game Center account, do any of the following:
   - *Remove friends:* Select one or more players in the list, then click the Remove button.

     When you remove a player from your list, you're also removed from their list. If you play them again, you're added back to each other's lists.
   - *Change your gaming nickname:* Click Details, then enter a new nickname or click a suggested nickname. Your nickname identifies you in games and is visible to other players.

- *Allow nearby players to invite you to a multiplayer game:* Click Details, then select Allow nearby Multiplayer. If you don't want to be found, deselect the checkbox.

  Nearby players are those on the same Wi-Fi network as you, or within Bluetooth range.

When you're signed in with the same Apple ID on all your Apple devices, your Game Center account is available on all the devices.

See game statistics and challenges

Most single player and multiplayer games show achievements and leaderboards so you can track your scores and ranking, and let you challenge other players to match or beat your statistics.

When you're in a game, look for buttons or menu items to view and share achievements, leaderboards, and challenges.

Play multiplayer games

- *Let a game find other players:* If the game provides Auto-match, click Play Now to let the game find other players for you.
- *Play nearby players:* If the game detects nearby players who are on the same Wi-Fi network as you, or

within Bluetooth range, it shows them. In the game, select a player.

- *Invite friends to play:* In the game, click Invite Friends, then select people from your contacts, friends, or nearby players. Customize your invitation, if you want, then click Send. You can send your invitation as a message, or send it to a phone number using SMS.
- *Accept an invitation:* In the notification or message, click Accept. The game opens (if you have it) so you can start playing. If you don't have the game, the App Store opens so you can get the game.

You can remove friends from the list in your Game Center account in Internet Accounts.

Note: You may receive notifications that let you know you're invited to join a game or that it's your turn to play in a turn-based game. Use Notifications preferences to ensure you receive games notifications or to stop or pause them.

Host and play sessions

A session is an iCloud-based game where up to 100 people can play at the same time, even forming teams to compete against each other. Because the game data is stored in iCloud instead of on your Mac, you can come and go in the game whenever you want.

You must be signed in with your Apple ID to host and play sessions.

- *Host a session:* When you invite friends to play a game that supports sessions, the session game data is stored using your iCloud storage.
- *Invite friends:* Depending on the game, you can invite people in your contacts using different methods, such as message or email.
- *Accept an invitation:* In the notification or message, click the session URL to accept the invitation. The game opens (if you have it) so you can start playing. If you don't have the game, the App Store opens so you can get the game.
- *End a session you're hosting:* You can end a session at any time; when you do, the game data is deleted from your iCloud storage.

  If a session is inactive for 6 months, it's automatically ended and the game data is deleted.

The administrator of a Mac can prevent other users of the Mac from joining multiplayer games or adding friends. The Game Center service may not be available in all areas.

Make music in GarageBand on Mac

GarageBand puts a complete music studio on your Mac, so you can make your own music to share with the world. You can create songs, ringtones, podcasts, and other types of projects in GarageBand. You can also learn to play your guitar or keyboard using the lessons included with GarageBand.

GarageBand comes on every new Mac.

If GarageBand isn't already installed on your Mac, you can get it from the Mac App Store.

Import, edit, and share movies in iMovie on Mac

Use iMovie to import your home videos from your camera. Then you can organize your videos, create movies and movie trailers, and share your movies right in iMovie.

IMovie comes on every new Mac.

If iMovie isn't already installed on your Mac, you can get it from the Mac App Store.

Chapter 9

Privacy and Security

Learn how passwords are used on

MacOS is designed to give you a safe and secure computing environment. The security of your Mac depends a great deal on using secure passwords in key areas.

Login password

A login password, also called a *user password*, allows you to log in and access the information on your Mac. When you create your login password, be sure it's easily memorable, write it down, and keep it in a secure location. Privileges are limited by the type of user. An administratoruser is required to perform many important tasks, such as setting certain system preferences, installing software, and administering standard users.

Apple ID

An Apple ID gives you access to the iTunes Store, the App Store, Apple Books, iCloud, FaceTime, and other Apple services. It consists of an email address (for example, michael_cavanna@icloud.com) and a password. Apple recommends you use the same Apple ID for all Apple services. When you create your Apple ID password, be sure it's easily memorable, write it down, and keep it in a secure location. You can also use your Apple ID to reset your login password if you forget it. Sign in to your Apple ID account page.

Passwords in iCloud Keychain

Keeping track of passwords is hard, especially if you follow the best practice of never using the same password twice and have multiple devices. ICloud Keychain keeps website and Wi-Fi passwords up to date across your Mac, iOS devices, and iPadOS devices. It also keeps account passwords and settings that you add to Internet Accounts preferences up to date on your Mac.

When you need to create a new password for a website, Safari suggests a unique, hard-to-guess password and saves it in your iCloud Keychain. Safari fills it in automatically the next time you need to sign in, so you don't have to remember it or enter it on any of your devices. It's recommended that you use the suggested strong password presented by Safari when creating passwords for websites and internet apps. If you don't use a suggested strong password and need help with a password for a website later, see the website's help, or the account information on the website.

If you need help with a password for an app that connects to an account on the internet or a network, see the documentation that came with the app, or online information that supports the app. For example, if you have a mail account with a service provider or website, see the documentation on the website or contact the provider.

Passwords in Keychain Access

Keychain Access stores passwords for various apps and services, and saves you the effort of authenticating separately for each of the items in your keychain. The keychain is secured by a keychain password, which is unlocked when a user logs in.

Recovery key

When you encrypt the information on your Mac using File Vault, you can create a recovery key. If you forget your login password, you can use the recovery key to unlock your startup disk and change the login password. The recovery key should not be stored in the same location as the Mac, where it can be discovered.

Manage passwords using keychains on Mac

MacOS uses keychains to help you keep track of and protect the passwords, account numbers, and other confidential information you use every day on your Mac computers and iOS and iPadOS devices.

You can use the Keychain Access app on your Mac to view and manage your keychains. When you use iCloud Keychain, you can keep your passwords and other secure information updated across your devices.

What is a keychain?

A keychain is an encrypted container that securely stores your account names and passwords for your Mac, apps, servers, and websites, and confidential information, such as credit card numbers or bank account PIN numbers.

When you access a website, email account, network server, or other password-protected item, you can choose to save the password in your keychain so you don't have to remember or enter the password each time.

Each user on a Mac has a login keychain. The password for your login keychain matches the password you use to log in to your Mac. If an administrator on your Mac resets your login password, you'll need to reset your login keychain password.

Keychain Access

You use the Keychain Access app on your Mac to view and manage your login and other keychains, and also the items securely stored in the keychains—for example, keys, certificates, passwords, account information, and notes. If you forget a password, you can find it in Keychain Access.

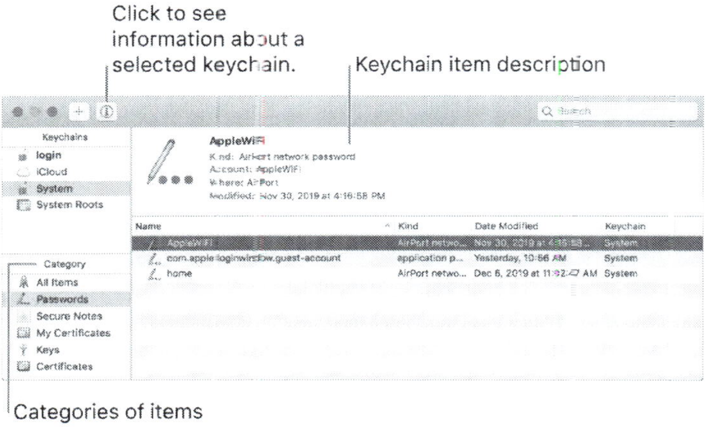

ICloud Keychain

If you use iCloud, you can have iCloud Keychain securely store the website login information and credit card information you use with AutoFill in Safari, and your Wi-Fi network information. ICloud Keychain automatically keeps that information up to date across all your Mac computers and iOS and iPadOS devices. ICloud Keychain also stores login information for the accounts you use in Mail, Contacts, Calendar, and Messages so it's available on all your devices.

Tip: When you use passwords and credit cards online, you can let Safari store them in your keychain and automatically fill them in for you. If you also use iCloud Keychain on your Mac and iOS and iPadOS devices, Safari can fill in the stored information on any of your devices.

Reset your Mac login password

Sometimes a login password needs to be reset—for example, if you have forgotten the login password and can't use a password hint to remember it.

When a user's login password is reset, a new default keychain is created to store the user's passwords.

Reset your login password using your Apple ID

If you associated your user account with your Apple ID, you can use your Apple ID to reset your login password.

1. On your Mac, choose Apple menu > Restart, or press the Power button on your computer and then click Restart.

2. Click your user account, click the question mark in the password field, then click the arrow next to "reset it using your Apple ID."
3. Enter an Apple ID and password, then click next.

   Follow the instructions to reset your login password.

Reset your login password using a recovery key

If you turned on File Vault encryption and created a recovery key, you can use the recovery key to reset your login password.

1. On your Mac, choose Apple menu > Restart, or press the Power button on your computer and then click Restart.
2. Click your user account, click the question mark in the password field, then click the arrow next to "reset it using your recovery key."
3. Enter the recovery key, then click next.

   Follow the instructions to reset your login password.

Reset the password of another user

An administrator can reset the passwords of other users.

1. On your Mac, choose Apple menu > System Preferences, then click Users & Groups.

2. Click the lock icon to unlock it, then enter an administrator name and password.
3. Select a user, then click Reset Password.

Set up your Mac to be secure

Here are some things you can do to make your Mac more secure.

Use secure passwords

To keep your information safe, you should use passwords to secure your Mac, and choose passwords that can't be easily guessed.

Require users to log in

If others can get physical access to your Mac, you should set up separate users for each person using the Mac, and require each user to log in. This prevents an unauthorized person from using the Mac. It also separates user files, so users only have access to their own personal files and settings. Users cannot see or modify the files or settings of other users.

Secure your Mac when it's idle

You can set your Mac to log out the current user if the Mac has been inactive for a certain period of time. You should also require a password to wake it from sleep or from the screen saver. For convenience, you can set up a hot corner to click whenever you want to immediately lock your screen.

Limit the number of administrative users

One or more people can have administrator privileges for a Mac. By default the administrator is the person who initially set up the Mac.

Administrators can create, manage, and delete other users, install and remove software, and change settings. For these reasons, an administrator should create a standard user account to use when administrator privileges are not needed. If the security of a standard user is compromised, the potential harm is far more limited than if the user has administrator privileges. If multiple people use your Mac, limit the number of users with administrator privileges.

Encrypt the data on your Mac with File Vault

If you have private or confidential information on your Mac, you can use File Vault encryption to protect that information from being seen or copied. File Vault encodes the information stored on your Mac so it is locked and cannot be read unless the login password is entered.

Guard your privacy on Mac

Privacy is an important concern when using apps that exchange information across the internet. MacOS includes security features to enhance your privacy and control the amount of information that's exposed about you and your Mac over the internet.

Use Screen Time

You can use Screen Time to monitor your children's computer use and limit their access to websites

Choose Apple menu > System Preferences, then click Screen Time.

Use the privacy features in Safari

Safari provides numerous features to help you control your privacy on the internet. You can browse privately, so Safari doesn't keep a record of websites you visited or items you downloaded. You can block pop-up windows, stop sites from storing cookies on your Mac, and more.

Control the personal information you share with apps

Location Services lets apps, such as web browsers, gather and use information based on your location. You can turn off Location Services completely, or you can select which apps can see information about your location.

Some apps may gather and use information from your contacts, photos, calendar, or reminders. Some apps may access the microphone or camera on your Mac.

Choose whether to share analytics information

You can help Apple improve the quality and performance of its products and services. MacOS can automatically collect analytics information from your Mac and send it to Apple for analysis. The information is sent only with your consent and is submitted anonymously to Apple. To choose whether analytics data is sent to Apple, use the Privacy pane of Security & Privacy preferences.

Choose Apple menu > System Preferences, click Security & Privacy, click Privacy, and then click Analytics.

Set up a firewall

You can use a firewall to protect your privacy by blocking unwanted network communications with your Mac. If the firewall is turned on, you can also use "stealth mode," which prevents your Mac from being discovered by others on the web.

To set up and customize your firewall, use the Firewall pane of Security & Privacy preferences.

Choose Apple menu > System Preferences, click Security & Privacy, then click Firewall.

Protect your Mac from malware

MacOS has many features that help protect your Mac and your personal information from malicious software, or malware. One common way malware is distributed is by embedding it in a harmless-looking app.

You can reduce this risk by using software only from reliable sources. The settings in Security & Privacy preferences allow you to specify the sources of software installed on your Mac.

1. On your Mac, choose Apple menu > System Preferences, click Security & Privacy, then click General.

2. Click the lock icon to unlock it, then enter an administrator name and password.

3. Select the sources from which you'll allow software to be installed:

   - *App Store:* Allows apps only from the Mac App Store. This is the most secure setting. All the developers of apps in the Mac App Store are identified by Apple, and each app is reviewed before it's accepted. MacOS checks the app before it opens the first time to be certain it hasn't been modified since the developer shipped it. If there's ever a problem with an app, Apple removes it from the Mac App Store.

- *App Store and identified developers:* Allows apps from the Mac App Store and apps from identified developers. Identified developers are registered with Apple and can optionally upload their apps to Apple for a security check. If problems occur with an app, Apple can revoke its authorization. MacOS checks the app before it opens the first time to be certain it hasn't been modified since the developer shipped it.

In addition to apps, other types of files may not be safe. Scripts, web archives, and Java archives have the potential to cause harm to your system. Of course, not all files like this are unsafe, but you should exercise caution when opening any such downloaded file. An alert appears when you first try to open these files.

Use Sign in with Apple on Mac

Sign in with Apple uses your Apple IDto securely create an account with an app or website—no need to fill out a form, verify your email address, or choose a new password—and simplifies signing in each time.

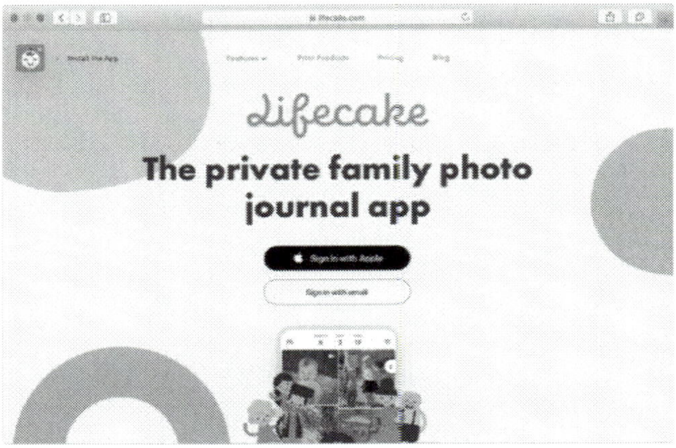

Create an account for an app or website

1. On your Mac, when you're asked to create an account for an app or a website, click Sign in with Apple, if available.
2. Follow the onscreen instructions, keeping the following in mind:
   - If you don't want to use your real name, click the Name field, then enter a different name.
   - If you have more than one email address associated with your Apple ID in Apple ID preferences, choose which email to use for the app or website.
   - If you prefer to keep your email address private, click Hide My Email. Apple generates a random and unique email address that's used

to forward emails from the app or website to your real email address.

Sign in to your account for an app or website

1. On your Mac, click Sign in with Apple.
2. Enter your login password on your Mac (you may need to enter your Apple ID password instead) or, if you're Mac has Touch ID, use Touch ID.

You can also sign in from your other devices—iPhone, iPad, Apple Watch, and Apple TV—where you're signed in with the same Apple ID.

Change the address used to forward email from apps and websites

If you chose to hide your email when you created an account, and you have more than one email address associated with your Apple ID in Apple ID preferences, you can change the address that receives forwarded email.

1. On your Mac, choose Apple menu > System Preferences, then click Apple ID.
2. In the sidebar, click "Name, Phone, Email," then click Edit next to Hide My Email.
3. Choose a different email address, then click done.

Change Sign in with Apple settings for an app or website

1. On your Mac, choose Apple menu > System Preferences, then click Apple ID.
2. In the sidebar, click Password & Security, then click Edit next to Apps Using Your Apple ID.
3. Click an app or website in the sidebar, then do any of the following:
    - *Turn off forwarding email:* Click Turn Off. You won't receive any further emails from the app or website.
    - *Stop using Sign in with Apple:* Click Stop Using Apple ID. You may be asked to create a new account the next time you try to sign in with the app or website.

Clear your browsing history in Safari on Mac

You can remove all records that Safari keeps of where you've browsed during a period of time you choose. If your Mac and your other devices have Safari turned on in iCloud preferences, your browsing history is removed from all of them. Clearing your browsing history in Safari doesn't clear any browsing histories kept independently by websites you visited.

1. In the Safari app on your Mac, choose History > Clear History, then click the pop-up menu.
2. Choose how far back you want your browsing history cleared.

When you clear your history, Safari removes data it saves as a result of your browsing, including:

- History of webpages you visited
- The back and forward list for open webpages
- Top Sites that aren't marked as permanent
- Frequently visited site list
- Recent searches
- Icons for webpages
- Snapshots saved for open webpages
- List of items you downloaded (downloaded files aren't removed)
- Websites added for Quick Website Search
- Websites that asked to use your location
- Websites that asked to send you notifications
- Websites with plug-in content you started by clicking a Safari Power Saver notice.

Manage cookies and website data in Safari on Mac

You can change options in Safari preferences so that Safari always accepts or always blocks cookies and website data.

In the Safari app on your Mac, choose Safari > Preferences, click Privacy, then do any of the following:

- *Prevent trackers from using cookies and website data to track you:* Select "Prevent cross-site tracking."

  Cookies and website data are deleted unless you visit and interact with the trackers' websites.

- *Always block cookies:* Select "Block all cookies."

  Websites, third parties, and advertisers can't store cookies and other data on your Mac. This may prevent some websites from working properly.

- *Remove stored cookies and data:* Click Manage Website Data, select one or more websites, then click Remove or Remove All.

  Removing the data may reduce tracking, but may also log you out of websites or change website behavior.

- *See which websites store cookies or data:* Click Manage Website Data.

Note: Changing your cookie preferences or removing cookies and website data in Safari may change or remove them in other apps.

Locate a device in Find My on Mac

In Find my, you can see the location of a missing device, and play a sound on it to help you find it.

Important: To be able to locate a missing device, you must add it in Find My before it's lost.

See the location of a device

1. In the Find My app on your Mac, click Devices.
2. In the Devices list, select the device you want to locate.
   - *If the device can be located:* It appears on the map so you can see where it is.
   - *If the device can't be located:* Below the device's name, "No location found" appears. If you want to be notified when the location is available, click the Info button on the map, then select Notify When Found. You receive a notification once it's located.

Play a sound on a device

1. In the Find My app on your Mac, click Devices.

2. In the Devices list, select the device you want to play a sound on, then click the Info button on the map.
3. Click Play Sound. For Air Pods, if they're separated, you can click Left or Right to find them one at a time.
    - *If the device is online:* A sound starts after a short delay and gradually increases in volume, then plays for about two minutes. The device may also vibrate. For all devices except Air Pods, a Find My [*device*] alert also appears on the device's screen.
    - *If the device is offline:* For Air Pods, you receive a notification on your devices the next time your Air Pods are in range of one of your devices and the Find My app is open. For all other devices, the sound plays the next time the device connects to a Wi-Fi or cellular network.

If you find your device, you can turn off the sound before it stops automatically—just press any button or any key.

Get directions to a device

1. In the Find My app on your Mac, click Devices.

2. In the Devices list, select the device you want to get directions to, then click the Info button on the map.
3. Click Directions.

   The Maps app opens with the directions from your location to the device's current location.

Chapter 10

Mac Hardware

Use trackpad and mouse gestures on Mac

When you use an Apple trackpad or a Magic Mouse with your Mac, you can use gestures—such as click, tap, pinch, and swipe—to zoom in on documents, browse through music or webpages, rotate photos, open Notification Center, and more.

Trackpad gestures

Use one or more fingers on the surface of your trackpad to click, tap, slide, swipe, and more. For example, to move between pages of a document, swipe left or right with two fingers. To see all of the trackpad gestures you can use with your Mac, or to turn off or customize gestures, choose Apple menu > System Preferences, then click Trackpad.

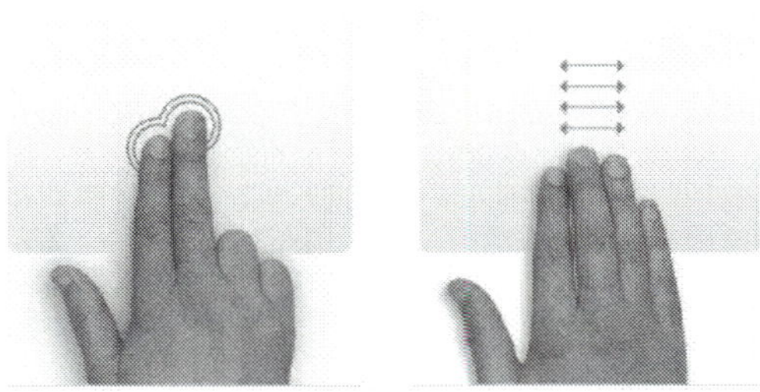

Zoom in and out of a webpage

Move between full-screen apps

Mouse gestures

Depending on the type of display connected to your Mac, you may also see a Contrast slider that you can use to adjust the display's contrast.

Set brightness from the menu bar

On some newer portable computers, you can help optimize battery use by setting the display brightness to approximately 75%. You see this option in the menu bar only when the display's brightness is set to a level that uses a significant amount of energy.

- On your Mac, click the battery icon in the menu bar, then click Display Brightness.

Note: If you don't see the battery icon in the menu bar, you need to show the battery's status.

You can't adjust the brightness of some older Apple displays. In OS X 10.10 and later, the Brightness slider may no longer appear in the Display pane of Displays preferences.

For specific information about the brightness of your display, check the documentation that came with your display.

Use the built-in camera on Mac

Many Mac computers and displays have a built-in insight, FaceTime, or FaceTime HD camera located near the top edge of the screen. The camera automatically turns on when you open an app that can take pictures, record videos, or make video calls. You can decide which apps are allowed to use the camera on your Mac. *Turn the camera on:* On your Mac, open an app that can use the camera, such as FaceTime, Messages, or Photo Booth. A green light beside the camera glows to indicate that the camera is on.

- *Turn the camera off:* On your Mac, close or quit all apps that can use the camera. The green light beside the camera turns off, showing that the camera is off.

Use Bluetooth devices with Mac

Bluetooth lets you make short-range wireless connections (up to 30 feet) between your Mac and devices such as mobile phones and peripherals.

Use the Bluetooth pane of System Preferences to connect to other Bluetooth devices. On your Mac, choose Apple menu > System Preferences, then click Bluetooth.

With Bluetooth you can:

- Use a wireless keyboard, mouse, or trackpad
- Use a Bluetooth headset with your computer
- Share files using Bluetooth
- Use a Bluetooth enabled printer

- Connect to the internet with a Bluetooth enabled phone

Connect an Apple wireless accessory with Mac

To use your Apple wireless keyboard, mouse, or trackpad, you first need to connect the device with your Mac to enable Bluetooth.

Connect a Magic Keyboard, Magic Mouse 2, or Magic Trackpad 2 with your Mac

When you connect your keyboard, mouse, or trackpad to your Mac, it automatically connects with the Mac using Bluetooth.

- Connect one end of a Lightning to USB Cable to your Magic Keyboard, Magic Mouse 2, or Magic Trackpad 2 and the other end to the USB port on your Mac. Depending on your Mac, you may need an adapter, which is available from an Apple Store or on apple.com.

  You can use your Magic Keyboard or Magic Trackpad 2 while it's connected to your Mac. You can't use your Magic Mouse 2 while it's connected.

When you use Bluetooth to connect your keyboard, mouse, or trackpad with your Mac, you receive a notification that you can disconnect the cable and use your device wirelessly.

Connect an Apple Wireless Keyboard, Magic Mouse, or Magic Trackpad with your Mac

Make sure the batteries are charged and properly inserted in the keyboard, mouse, or trackpad and the device is turned on and discoverable.

1. On your Mac, choose Apple menu > System Preferences, then click Bluetooth.
2. Select the keyboard, mouse, or trackpad in the Devices list, then click Connect.

If you replace the batteries in a keyboard, mouse, or trackpad, click the mouse or trackpad or press a key on the keyboard to reconnect it with your Mac.

For more help using Bluetooth, click the Help button ? in Bluetooth preferences.

Connect a display, TV, or projector to Mac

You can connect your Mac to a display, TV, or projector using one or more of these options.

- *Connect a display to a USB-C port:* Use a Thunderbolt 3 (USB-C) cable to connect the display to the USB-C port on your Mac. For older displays, use a USB-C Digital AV Multiport Adapter or a USB-C VGA Multiport Adapter to connect the display to the USB-C port on your Mac.

- *Connect a display, TV, or projector that has an HDMI connector:* Plug the cable directly into the HDMI port on your Mac. For more information about connecting a TV, *Connect a display or projector that has a VGA connector:* Use a Mini DisplayPort to VGA Adapter to connect the display to the Thunderbolt port on your Mac.
- *Connect a display to a Mini DisplayPort:* Plug the display's cable directly into the Mini DisplayPort on your Mac.
- *Connect an Apple Thunderbolt Display:* Plug the display's cable directly into the Thunderbolt port on your Mac. For newer Mac computers, use a Thunderbolt 3 (USB-C) to Thunderbolt 2 Adapter to connect the display to your Mac.
- *Connect an Apple LED Cinema Display:* Plug the display's cable directly into the Mini DisplayPort or Thunderbolt 2 port on your Mac. For newer Mac computers, use a Thunderbolt 3 (USB-C) to Thunderbolt 2 adapter to connect the display to your Mac.

If your display uses a video port that's not available on your Mac, you may be able to use an adapter to connect your display.

Burn CDs and DVDs on Mac

If your Mac has a built-in optical drive, or if you connect an external DVD drive (for example, an Apple USB SuperDrive), you can burn files to CDs and DVDs to share your files with friends, move files between computers, or create backup files. Discs you burn on your Mac can also be used on Windows and other types of computers.

1. Insert a blank disc into your optical drive.

   If you see a dialog, click the pop-up menu, then choose Open Finder. Select "Make this action the default" if you want to open the Finder every time you insert a blank disc.

   The disc appears on your desktop.

2. Double-click the disc to open its window, then drag the files and folders you want to burn to the window.

   Aliases to the files are placed in the disc's window. The original files are not moved or deleted.

   Note: If you want to burn the same files to discs multiple times, use a burn folder.

3. Arrange and rename the files.

When the disc is burned, the items on the disc have the same names and locations that they have in the disc window. After the disc is burned, you can't change the items.

4. Choose File > Burn [*disc*], then follow the instructions.

   The files that the aliases point to are burned to the disc. In addition, if the folders you add to the disc contain aliases, the files those aliases point to are also burned to the disc.

   Note: If you eject the disc without burning it, a burn folder with the items you copied to the disc is created and placed on your desktop. To complete the burn process, click the burn icon  next to the folder in the Finder sidebar, or press and hold the Control key as you click any disc, then choose Burn Disc from the shortcut menu.

To burn a disc image (.dmg file) to a disc, Control-click the disc image file, choose "Burn Disc Image [*disc name*] to Disc" from the shortcut menu, then follow the instructions.

Tip: To erase the contents of a rewritable disc, Control-click the CD or DVD drive in the Finder sidebar, then choose Erase Rewriteable Disc from the shortcut menu.

Optimize storage space on your Mac

MacOS can help make more room on your Mac by optimizing its storage. When space is needed, it keeps files, photos and videos, Apple TV movies and shows, and email attachments in iCloud and makes them available on demand. Files don't take up space on your Mac, and you can download the original files when you need them. Recent files and optimized versions of your photos are always on your Mac.

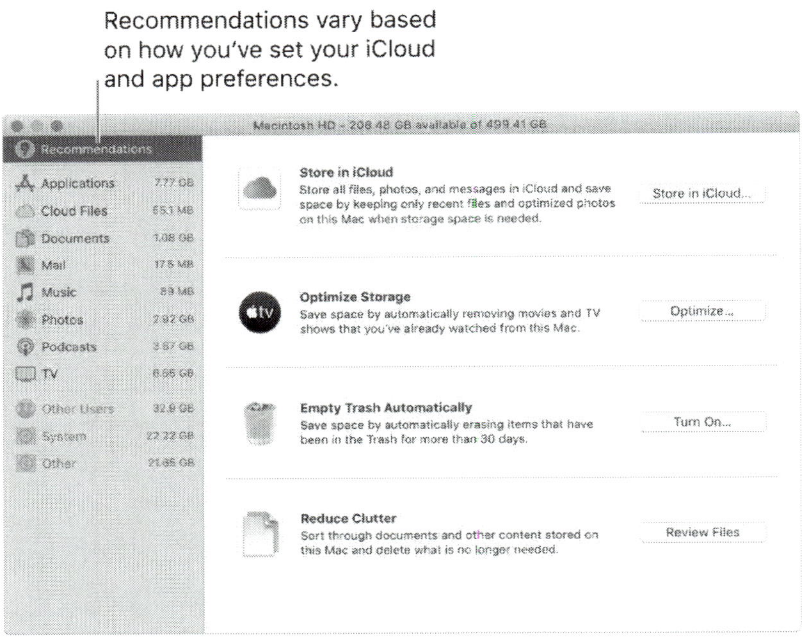

1. Choose Apple menu > About This Mac, click Storage, then click Manage.

   MacOS calculates how much space is being used by different categories.

Note: Wait until all categories are finished being calculated to ensure you're seeing the accurate amount of space. Values are refined as each category is calculated.

2. View the recommendations and decide how to optimize storage on your Mac.

Thank you for purchasing our user guide!

Printed in Great Britain
by Amazon

35302536R00170